GMDSS
A USER'S HANDBOOK

WELL – IT'S DEFINITELY A MAYDAY –
BUT IS IT 'FIRE' OR 'SINKING'?

4th edition **GMDSS**
A USER'S HANDBOOK
DENISE BRÉHAUT

ADLARD COLES NAUTICAL
LONDON

FOR JAKE, MY FRIEND,
MY HERO AND MY SAFE HAVEN.

Published by Adlard Coles Nautical
an imprint of A & C Black Publishers Ltd
36 Soho Square, London W1D 3QY
www.adlardcoles.com

First edition 1999
Second edition 2002
Third edition 2006
Fourth edition 2009

ISBN 978-1408-11493-3

A CIP catalogue record for this book is available from the British Library.

This book is produced using paper that is made from wood grown in managed, sustainable
forests. It is natural, renewable and recyclable. The logging and manufacturing processes
conform to the environmental regulations of the country of origin.

Cartoon on page i by Jake Kavanagh

Typeset in 10 on 12pt URWGroteskTLig
Printed and bound in Spain by GraphyCems

Note: While all reasonable care has been taken in the preparation of this publication, the
publisher takes no responsibility for the use of the methods or products described in the book.

CONTENTS

PREFACE

In 1988 The Global Maritime Distress and Safety System (GMDSS) was incorporated into the 1974 Safety Of Life At Sea (SOLAS) regulations. This 1988 amendment came into force on 1 February 1992 and became mandatory from 1 February 1999 for compulsorily fitted craft. These are vessels over 300 GRT and passenger vessels on international voyages.

In the transition the percentage of false distress alerts rose to 96%. A false distress alert is one that has been inadvertently sent. Many of these can be directly attributed to poorly designed equipment and lack of sufficient training. Radio Officers are no longer being trained. In many cases, the responsibility for communications has been added to that of the Deck Officer.

Equipment design is being addressed by the introduction of more specific guidelines for manufacturers. There is no plan to recall the preceding generations of equipment already installed on board vessels. However, the International Maritime Organization (IMO) is urging the use of dedicated protected distress buttons and modification of existing equipment where necessary. Training courses are intensive, making it possible to instruct students on only one or two designs of equipment, and moreover course providers often have the most up-to-date equipment. It is, therefore, imperative to stress that users, once qualified, should take the time to read their instruction manuals and learn how to use the specific equipment on board their vessels. Diligence and awareness can decrease the false alert rate.

Class D VHF Digital Selective Calling (DSC) controllers have been produced for leisure craft and other voluntarily fitted vessels in coastal waters whose owners wish to benefit from the GMDSS. These units are much less complex than those produced for the merchant shipping market. However, it is just as important to gain training and an insight into the system as a whole to ensure that distress alerts are not sent in error.

Examination syllabi for the GMDSS General Operator Certificate (GOC), Long Range Certificate (LRC) and Restricted Operator Certificate (ROC) are covered within this book, as simply as possible. Although the text covers more detail than is required for the ROC examination, it is hoped that readers will gain a valuable insight into the system as a whole. Candidates embarking on GOC and LRC training courses will benefit greatly from reading the text in advance. It can then be used as a reference book during the course and an aide memoire once qualified.

GLOSSARY OF ABBREVIATIONS

AIS-SART	Automatic Identification System – Search And Rescue Transmitter
ALRS	Admiralty List of Radio Signals
AMVER	Automated Mutual-Assistance VEssel Rescue System
AORE	Atlantic Ocean Region East
AORW	Atlantic Ocean Region West
ATU	Antenna Tuning Unit
CRS	Coast Radio Station
CS	Coast Station
CQ	An abbreviation for All Stations
DE	An abbreviation for This Is
DMG	Distress Message Generator
DSC	Digital Selective Calling
EGC	Enhanced Group Calling
EPIRB	Emergency Position Indicating Radio Beacon
EU	Electronic Unit
FEC	Forward Error Correction (telex mode used for Navtex)
GHz	Gigahertz (1000 MHz)
GMDSS	Global Maritime Distress and Safety System
GPS	Global Positioning System
GRT	Gross Registered Tonnage
H24	Continuous service
H3E	Single sideband with full carrier
HF	High Frequency 3–30 MHz (Marine HF 4–27.5 MHz)
HX	No fixed hours or specific intermittent hours
IMO	International Maritime Organization
IOR	Indian Ocean Region
ITU	International Telecommunications Union
J3E	Single sideband with suppressed carrier
kHz	Kilohertz
LES	Land Earth Station (can be called a Coast Earth Station)
LUT	Local User Terminal
MCA	Maritime and Coastguard Agency
MCC	Mission Control Centre
MES	Mobile Earth Station (can be called a Ship Earth Station)
MF	Medium Frequency 300–3000 kHz (Marine MF 1.6–4 MHz)
MHz	Megahertz
MID	Maritime Identification Digits
MMSI	Maritime Mobile Service Identity
MRCC	Maritime Rescue Co-ordination Centre
MSI	Maritime Safety Information
NCS	Network Co-ordination Station
NOAA	National Oceanic and Atmospheric Administration
POR	Pacific Ocean Region
PTT	Press To Talk

R3E	Single sideband with reduced pilot carrier
RT	RadioTelephony – ie voice communications
Rx	Receiver
SAR	Search And Rescue
SART	Search And Rescue Transponder
SOLAS	Safety Of Life At Sea
SSB	Single SideBand
TDM	Time-Division Multiplexing
Tx	Transmitter
UTC	Universal Time, Co-ordinated
VHF	Very High Frequency 30–300 MHz (Marine VHF 156–174 MHz)

ACKNOWLEDGEMENTS

My thanks to Kevin Walsh, Terry Slack, Jake Kavanagh and Marion Bréhaut for reading the manuscript.

Special thanks to Gill Norton, Stan Bréhaut, Marion Bréhaut, Jake Kavanagh, David Miller and Capt P Valentin for their time and encouragement.

Illustrations by Gill Norton.
Computer graphics by Stan Bréhaut.
Photographs by Denise Bréhaut.
Thank you to all concerned for providing photo opportunities.

SafetyNET and FleetNET are service marks of INMARSAT.

Chapter 1

INTRODUCTION TO THE SYSTEMS

In 1979 the International Maritime Organisation (IMO) Assembly overviewed the existing maritime distress and safety system. In the light of technological advances, it was decided to create a new Global Maritime Distress and Safety System (GMDSS) to improve the safety of life at sea.

The old system was based on coast stations and certain classes of vessels maintaining a continuous listening watch on nominated distress frequencies. These vessels were also required to carry basic communications equipment with a working range of approximately 150 nautical miles. Vessels in distress offshore were therefore reliant on nearby shipping to provide assistance.

The new system, which came into force in 1992, incorporated satellites and digital selective calling technology, enabling distress alerts to be received automatically over great distances.

Despite some students finding the new technology and procedures daunting, it is important to remember that the difference with GMDSS is that there are now more ways of alerting Maritime Rescue Co-ordination Centres (MRCC) and other authorities to a maritime incident (see Figure 1 on page 2). Many of these new options are more reliable than the old methods and because of the use of technologically advanced equipment, specialist knowledge is not required to operate it. You do not need to know how a TV recorder produces a copy of a television programme but it is imperative that you are able to program it to record a specific item or the technology is wasted. In the same way, you only need an understanding of the GMDSS, along with basic knowledge of how to operate the equipment relating to each system without sending false alerts.

Comparatively few years ago, the only means of calling for assistance at sea was by terrestrial VHF or MF radio. Small craft only had the option of VHF radio until the 1979 Fastnet disaster prompted the production of smaller long range communications equipment. In communications prior to 1999, satellites were only used for the Emergency Position Indicating Radio Beacon (EPIRB). Now the INMARSAT satellites enable near global communications whilst at sea. Digital Selective Calling (DSC), the latest introduction to the GMDSS, has provided a reliable means of terrestrial alerting. Today even the smallest craft can choose to participate in the GMDSS and benefit from improved communications and enhanced search and rescue facilities.

One major change has been the equipment requirements for compulsorily fitted vessels. The old regulations were designed around the size of the ship, with 300 GRT and 1600 GRT being the two main categories. In the GMDSS, trading areas determine

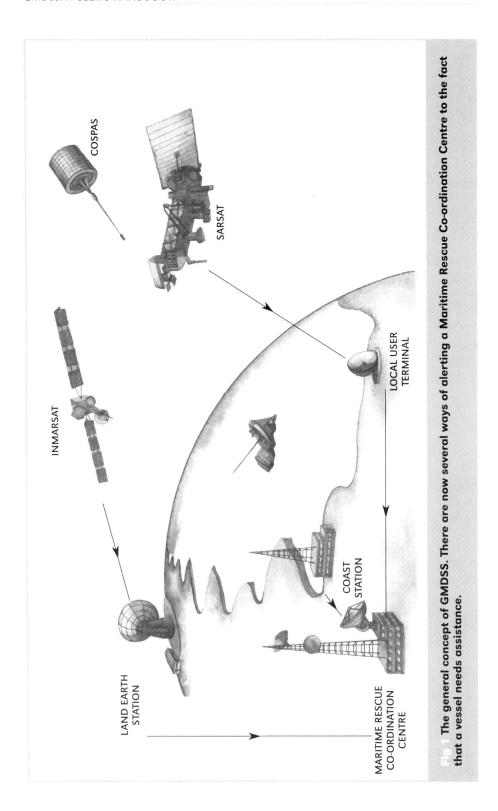

Fig 1 The general concept of GMDSS. There are now several ways of alerting a Maritime Rescue Co-ordination Centre to the fact that a vessel needs assistance.

the equipment requirements, not the size of the vessel. Sea areas one to four are used to define these trading areas (see Figure 2 for sea areas in north-west Europe).

SEA AREAS

A1 is an area within the radiotelephone coverage of at least one VHF coast station operating DSC equipment. Approximately 30–40 mile range.

A2 is an area within the radiotelephone coverage of at least one MF coast station operating DSC equipment, excluding A1 areas. Approximately 150 mile range.

A3 is an area within the coverage of at least one INMARSAT geostationary satellite (between 70° north and south), excluding A1 and A2 areas.

A4 covers the Polar Regions and excludes A1, A2 and A3 areas.

EQUIPMENT REQUIREMENTS FOR COMPULSORILY FITTED VESSELS

AREA A1

Vessels trading exclusively in an A1 area are required to carry a VHF transceiver with channels 16, 13, 06 and those suitable for public correspondence. In addition,

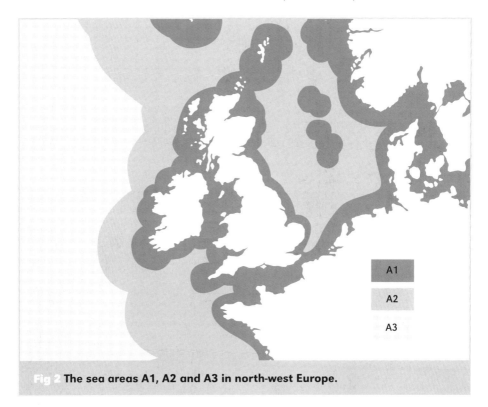

A1

A2

A3

Fig 2 The sea areas A1, A2 and A3 in north-west Europe.

they need DSC equipment that is capable of transmitting and watch keeping on channel 70.

AREA A2

Vessels trading in A2 areas are required to carry the A1 equipment plus an MF transceiver with 2182 kHz and public correspondence frequencies for telephone or telex. In addition, DSC equipment is required that is capable of transmitting and watch keeping on 2187.5 kHz.

AREA A3

Vessels trading in A3 areas are required to carry the A1 and A2 equipment plus one of the following options:

The INMARSAT option

Equipment is required that provides telex alerting, watch keeping and public correspondence by telex or telephone. INMARSAT C meets all of these requirements. Ships are now able to choose to trade deep sea without carrying HF radio equipment.

The HF option

This option requires the installation of an HF transceiver providing radiotelephony and radiotelex. In addition, an HF DSC controller is required with scanning watch keeping on 4207.5, 6312, 8414.5, 12577 and 16804.5 kHz.

AREA A4

Vessels trading in A4 areas are required to carry the equipment for areas A1, A2 and the A3 HF option.

ALL SEA AREAS

In addition to the above, all vessels are required to carry a Navtex receiver for the reception of Maritime Safety Information (MSI). If trading is primarily in an area outside the coverage of Navtex, MSI should be obtained through the INMARSAT SafetyNET service. All vessels should carry a satellite Emergency Position Indicating Radio Beacon (EPIRB) in a float free mounting, transmitting on 406 MHz. Two Search and Rescue Transponders (SARTs) are required, along with three handheld VHF radios if over 500 GRT and two if between 300 and 500 GRT.

VOLUNTARILY FITTED VESSELS

The fitting of GMDSS equipment to leisure craft is optional. However, all craft, regardless of size, are advised to carry a VHF radio. Handheld or transportable VHF radios are sufficient for very small craft staying within five nautical miles of land. They are also useful as an additional piece of safety equipment. Fixed VHF radios are advisable for larger vessels venturing further afield. The transmitter power output is greater and the aerial is higher, enabling communications at a greater range. A VHF DSC controller is a useful piece of equipment to carry and may even become essential once coast stations cease to keep a listening watch on channel 16. An EPIRB, SART, MF radio and MF DSC controller are advisable on board a vessel that may travel up to

150 nautical miles from a safe haven. INMARSAT systems may be considered by larger craft on longer passages as an alternative to HF radio. Navtex is a convenient way to receive weather and navigational information without listening to the various transmissions that are available from other sources.

QUESTIONS

1 To which vessels do the GMDSS regulations apply?

2 Define GMDSS sea area A1.

3 Define GMDSS sea area A2.

4 Define GMDSS sea area A3.

5 Define GMDSS sea area A4.

ANSWERS

1 The regulations apply to vessels over 300 GRT and passenger vessels on international voyages.

2 Sea area A1 is an area within the radiotelephone coverage of at least one VHF coast station operating DSC equipment. Approximately 30–40 mile range.

3 Sea area A2 is an area within the radiotelephone coverage of at least one MF coast station operating DSC equipment, excluding A1 areas. Approximately 150 mile range.

4 Sea area A3 is an area within the coverage of at least one INMARSAT geostationary satellite, excluding A1 and A2 areas.

5 Sea area A4 covers the Polar Regions and excludes A1, A2 and A3 areas.

Chapter 2

TRAINING COURSES AND EXAMINATIONS

THE GENERAL OPERATOR CERTIFICATE COURSE (GOC)

The GMDSS General Operator Certificate (GOC) is the most advanced of the courses covered within this text. In the UK, most course providers will offer either a straight seven-day course prior to the examination, or seven weekdays with the weekend free for private study. Any course will be intensive, with private study required in the evenings. Candidates will be at an advantage if they do some pre-course learning and have keyboard familiarity. A course is compulsory for access to the exam.

THE GOC EXAMINATION

The examination structure is constantly being reviewed and revised. The following information is a guide to the UK examination at the time of writing. It should also be noted that other administrations have different examination structures. There is a facility to upgrade an existing LRC operator's certificate to a GOC. The GOC examination consists of three sections:

1 THE GENERAL KNOWLEDGE PAPER

The paper comprises three SOLAS questions based on distress, urgency and safety. There are also 15 multi-choice questions about the radio regulations in general. There are 25 minutes in which to complete the paper. There are 15 marks available for each SOLAS answer and one for each multi-choice. Examiners strictly adhere to the marking scheme and the pass mark is 75%. This is one of the major stumbling blocks in the GOC examination and examination technique certainly plays a part.

2 THE RADIOTELEPHONY EXAMINATION

During the radiotelephony (RT) examination a simulation of RT working is conducted. Each candidate is required to respond to transmissions in the appropriate manner. At the same time, all candidates are required to keep radio logs. The examination lasts approximately 30 minutes for a group of eight candidates. The pass mark is 75%, with correct recording of positions in the log book being mandatory. With sufficient practice during the course, this examination should be fairly straightforward.

3 OPERATIONAL PERFORMANCE TEST

This is the practical test, which will be made as realistic as possible. The candidate will be joining a ship and be given a scenario. During the passage, the candidate will be asked to use the MF, HF and VHF transceivers, MF, HF and VHF DSC controllers, Navtex, INMARSAT Fleet F77 or INMARSAT B and INMARSAT C equipment. Knowledge of batteries, EPIRBs and SARTs, along with keyboard skills and the ability to use publications, are also tested. Each candidate is tested individually for up to 90 minutes. The pass mark is 70%, with no 'grey box' tick on the examiner's report. The examiner will award a 'grey box' tick and fail the candidate if, for instance, the candidate cannot switch on the piece of equipment or perform safety critical operations. Being scenario based, the duration of this examination is mainly determined by the candidate, however it is worth bearing in mind the 90 minute cut off time.

THE LONG RANGE CERTIFICATE COURSE (LRC)

The Long Range Certificate (LRC) replaces the old Restricted Certificate of Competence in Radiotelephony, often known as the SSB certificate. The LRC certificate is specific to the UK and has been tailored to meet the needs of the leisure market and commercial craft less than 300 GRT. In addition to the LRC, there is an optional satellite module. The LRC course typically lasts four days. Many course providers will offer a longer course.

THE LRC EXAMINATION

The examination consists of four sections:

1 THE SOLAS PAPER

This may be written or conducted orally. There are 12 questions about distress, urgency and safety. The duration of the paper is left to the examiner's discretion. The pass mark is 75%.

2 THE REGULATIONS PAPER

This may be written or conducted orally. The paper contains 10 multi-choice questions about the radio regulations in general. The duration of the paper is again left to the discretion of the examiner. The pass mark is 60%.

3 THE RADIOTELEPHONY EXAMINATION

This takes exactly the same format as the GOC examination above.

4 OPERATIONAL PERFORMANCE TEST

This is the practical test using the MF, HF and VHF transceivers, MF, HF and VHF DSC controllers and Navtex. Knowledge of EPIRBs, SARTs, batteries and antennae is also tested, along with the ability to use publications. The test is carried out on an individual basis and may last up to 45 minutes. The pass mark is 70%, with no 'grey box' tick.

SATELLITE MODULE

The satellite module consists of two sections that may be taken at the same time as the LRC examination, at no extra charge.

1 THE SOLAS PAPER

Five questions based on distress, urgency and safety. The pass mark is 60%.

2 THE OPERATIONAL PERFORMANCE TEST

This is a 15-minute practical test on the INMARSAT C transceiver. The pass mark is 71%, with no 'grey box' tick.

THE RESTRICTED OPERATOR CERTIFICATE COURSE (ROC)

The Restricted Operator Certificate was introduced in 1998. It provides a GMDSS qualification for commercial operators trading exclusively in A1 areas. Many course providers will offer a two- or three-day course prior to the examination.

THE ROC EXAMINATION

This examination consists of three sections:

1 THE SOLAS PAPER

This may be written or conducted orally. There are nine questions on distress, urgency and safety. The duration of the paper is left to the examiner's discretion. The pass mark is 75%.

2 THE REGULATIONS AND OPERATIONAL PERFORMANCE TEST

This covers the practical use of the equipment and oral questions on the regulations in general. Practical use of the VHF transceiver, VHF DSC controller, EPIRBs, SARTs and Navtex equipment will be tested. Knowledge of batteries and antennae is also tested, along with the ability to use publications. Each candidate is tested individually for up to 45 minutes. The pass mark is 75%, with no 'grey box' tick.

3 THE RADIOTELEPHONY EXAMINATION

This takes exactly the same format as the GOC examination above.

STCW

All officers who need to comply with the STCW code must have their ROC or GOC GMDSS certificate endorsed by the MCA. After obtaining the STCW endorsement, they must revalidate every 5 years. This is done by providing the relevant forms and proving at least 1 year of sea service in the last 5.

Chapter 3

MODES OF EMISSION AND PROPAGATION

There is no requirement to know radio communications theory in detail, either for the examinations or for practical use of the equipment. What follows is therefore a very simple explanation.

MODES OF EMISSION

When the Press To Talk (PTT) switch on the microphone is operated, a carrier is generated. Figure 3 shows the carrier on a frequency spectrum diagram. The vertical axis indicates power or level.

Fig 3 A carrier on a frequency spectrum.

If someone speaks into the microphone when the PTT is held in, voice modulation is superimposed onto each side of the carrier. This produces an upper and lower sideband, which are mirror images of each other and contain identical information. The transmitter power will be shared between the carrier and the sidebands. For example, a fully modulated 400 watt transmitter would radiate a carrier of 267 watts and 66.5 watts in each of the sidebands. The mode represented in Figure 4 is known as A3E, **double sideband with full carrier**.

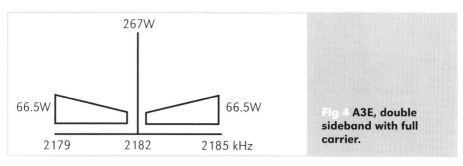

Fig 4 A3E, double sideband with full carrier.

The human ear can detect audio frequencies from approximately 20 to 25,000 Hz. However, only speech signals between approximately 300 Hz and 3000 Hz (3 kHz) are used in a maritime transmitter. Speech frequencies up to 3 kHz will produce intelligible communications but they will lack personality. As a result, the bandwidth of the modulated carrier is 6 kHz, 3 kHz for each sideband. If we take 2182 kHz as an example, a transmission will use frequencies from 2179 kHz to 2185 kHz, with 2182 kHz being the assigned frequency to which we refer.

We actually only need the upper sideband for maritime communications, so a filter is used from 2179 to 2181.9 kHz to remove the lower sideband. Remember that with the 400 watt transmitter, 267 watts are used to produce the carrier. The remaining 133 watts are now available for use by the upper sideband. The practical result of this is that either the drain on the ship's batteries can be reduced without significant loss of range, or the range of communications can be increased without increasing the power output of the transmitter (see Figure 5).

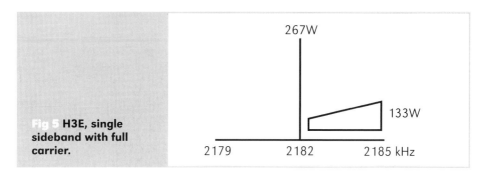

Fig 5 **H3E, single sideband with full carrier.**

This mode is known as H3E, **single sideband with full carrier**, sometimes labelled AM, and was always used by ships transmitting on 2182 kHz. This is the only mode that is compatible with A3E. Some survival craft radio equipment used A3E but it became obsolete with the full implementation of GMDSS. H3E is, therefore, no longer used on 2182 kHz.

The ideal situation would be to suppress the carrier completely, making all of the transmitter power available to the upper sideband; 66.5 watts would now produce the same effective radiated power as the original 400 watt transmission using A3E. The carrier must be generated in the transmitter in order to place the audio frequencies in the correct part of the radio frequency spectrum. Once this has been achieved, the carrier is removed by circuitry prior to transmission. The mode represented in Figure 6 is known as J3E, **single sideband with suppressed carrier**, sometimes labelled USB, now the most frequently used mode in maritime communications.

Fig 6 **J3E, single sideband with suppressed carrier.**

A receiver cannot detect radio frequency without a full carrier. Much of the expense of a communications receiver is in the circuitry that is necessary to reinsert the carrier. The reinsertion must be in exactly the same place as if the original transmitter had produced it. In some situations, especially with old equipment, a pilot may be needed in order to act as a guide for carrier reinsertion. This pilot is achieved by sending a small amount of carrier. The mode is known as R3E, **single sideband with reduced carrier**. This mode, represented in Figure 7, would only be selected if the receiving station requested it. However, most modern equipment is capable of receiving J3E without any real difficulty.

2179   2182   2185 kHz

Fig 7 **R3E, single sideband with reduced carrier.**

If the inserted carrier frequency is either too high or too low, the pitch of the received voice signal will be wrong (see Figure 8). The receiving station can modify the frequency of the carrier by use of the **clarifier** or **fine tune** control.

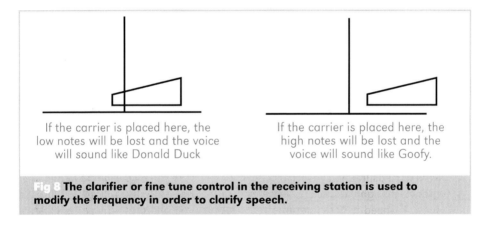

If the carrier is placed here, the low notes will be lost and the voice will sound like Donald Duck

If the carrier is placed here, the high notes will be lost and the voice will sound like Goofy.

Fig 8 **The clarifier or fine tune control in the receiving station is used to modify the frequency in order to clarify speech.**

The last modes that you need to know about are those used for radiotelex. F1B is used for radiotelex and DSC on MF and HF. It uses Frequency Shift Keying (FSK), with two carriers separated by just 170 Hz. J2B uses two audio tones to send telex over radio.

To help you to remember

A3E **A**ll of the carrier and **A**ll of the information.
H3E Was used on 2182 kHz, which was where we called for **H**elp. Uses the w**H**ole carrier and single sideband.
J3E **J**ust the single sideband, no carrier. Used **J**ust about all the time.
R3E **R**educed carrier, single sideband.

PROPAGATION OF THE RADIO WAVE

In free space, electromagnetic waves have both electric and magnetic fields that are always at right angles to each other and the direction of travel. The continual build-up and collapse of these fields is represented in Figure 9 by a sine wave. When the frequency of such electromagnetic waves is suitable for communications by radio, it is referred to as a radio wave. Radio waves travel outwards through the air at a constant speed of approximately 186,000 miles per second, which is the speed of light, in the form of an expanding sphere from an omnidirectional antenna. The wavelength is the distance between two points of repetition, usually measured in metres. The wavelength of 156.8 MHz (VHF channel 16), for example, is 1.91 metres and that of 2182 kHz is 137.5 metres.

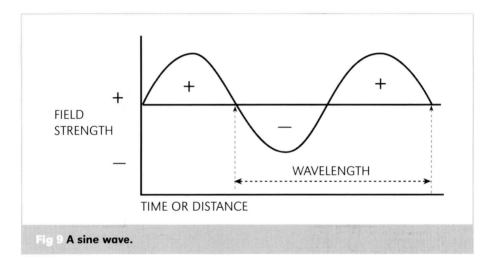

Fig 9 A sine wave.

The frequency is the number of waves that pass a given point in a given amount of time, usually measured in cycles per second or Hertz (Hz). The wavelength of channel 16 (VHF, Very High Frequency) is smaller than that of 2182 kHz (MF, Medium Frequency). If speed is constant, more 1.91 metre units will pass a given point in a given time than 137.5 metre units in the same time, therefore we can deduce that the frequency must be higher.

Some students find the relationship between kHz, MHz and GHz confusing.

To help you to remember

1 kHz = 1,000 Hz
1 MHz = 1,000 kHz = 1,000,000 Hz
1 GHz = 1,000 MHz = 1,000,000 kHz = 1,000,000,000 Hz
2182 kHz can also be referred to as being 2.182 MHz, in the 2 MHz band.

THE IONOSPHERE

The existence of ionised layers in the atmosphere was not realised until the 1920s, when radio communications over long distances were achieved using HF (High Frequency) propagation. These layers are now collectively called the ionosphere. As X-rays and ultraviolet radiation from the sun enter the upper atmosphere, they strip electrons from atoms and molecules present in these layers. The electrons are negatively charged and the remaining atoms become positively charged due to the loss of the electrons. These positively charged atoms are known as ions, hence the naming of the ionosphere. Due to the electromagnetic nature of radio waves, this charged layer can affect their propagation. The effect takes the form of refraction, meaning that radio waves entering the ionosphere will have their paths bent. If enough bending occurs, the wave will be refracted back to earth.

The distance covered between the transmitter and the point of possible reception of the returning wave in a single hop is known as the Skip Distance. The geographical area where the transmission cannot be received is called the Dead Zone. The higher the frequency of the radio wave, the more ions are required to refract it and return it to earth. As frequency increases, the amount of bending decreases and frequencies greater than approximately 30 MHz will penetrate the ionosphere relatively unaffected and escape into space (see Figure 10).

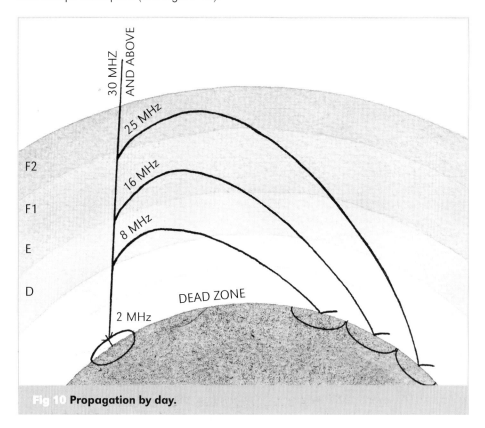

Fig 10 **Propagation by day.**

Three separate layers are recognisable within the ionosphere. The D layer occurs below 55 miles, the E layer between 55 and 100 miles and the F layer, which is subdivided into F1 and F2, above this altitude. These layers are not constant but fluctuate with, for example, time of day or season and are extremely variable during the 11-year sun spot cycle. When the sun's radiation is strong, HF propagation is better because there are more ions present in the ionosphere. Some stations produce propagation prediction charts that take these anomalies into consideration.

Since ionisation is primarily caused by incoming solar radiation, the number of free electrons and ions increases with altitude and decreases in all layers at night. Refraction at a higher level within the ionosphere will produce greater skip distances and also greater dead zones. The maritime community is allocated parts of the spectrum in the 4, 6, 8, 12, 16, 22 and 26 MHz bands. Each band will be affected differently by the ionosphere.

The F2 layer contains the highest ion density and refracts high HF radio waves. The F1 layer is less ionised and refracts radio waves in the mid HF range. The use of these layers will enable communications over approximately 2500 to 2000 miles respectively with one hop. At night the two layers combine to form a single F layer.

Within the E layer the ion density is lower still and is responsible for refracting lower HF frequencies, enabling communications over approximately 1500 miles with one hop.

The D layer is of special interest. The air itself is denser but contains the lowest level of ionisation. Frequencies below 3 MHz, which include MF radio waves, are weakened or disappear in this layer during the day due to the activity between the molecules of the air and the electrons. The D layer is most active around mid-day. However, at night, when there are fewer electrons, these waves can pass through unaffected, to be refracted in the layers above.

TYPES OF RADIO WAVES

Each radio transmission propagates in three distinct modes, one of which will always be dominant depending on the frequency involved. The three modes are a ground wave, a sky wave and a direct wave. Ground waves follow the curvature of the earth and because of their proximity to the ground they lose their energy to it, producing a usable range of approximately 150 to 200 miles. Slightly greater ranges may be achieved using an efficient long wire antenna. Long-distance communications are achieved by the use of sky waves that are refracted by the ionosphere and returned to earth. Several skips are possible, which will enable communications over many thousands of miles. Direct waves are used for communications over short distances, directly from one aerial to another.

GROUND WAVE

The ground wave range becomes shorter as frequency becomes higher. MF uses primarily the ground wave and the range is mainly dependent on transmitter power output. During the day, approximately one kilometre of range for every watt of radiated power can be expected. However, during the night, as we have seen, the sky wave can be used. 2182 kHz transmissions can therefore increase from around 150 miles during the day using the ground wave to about 1000 miles at night using the sky wave (see Figure 11).

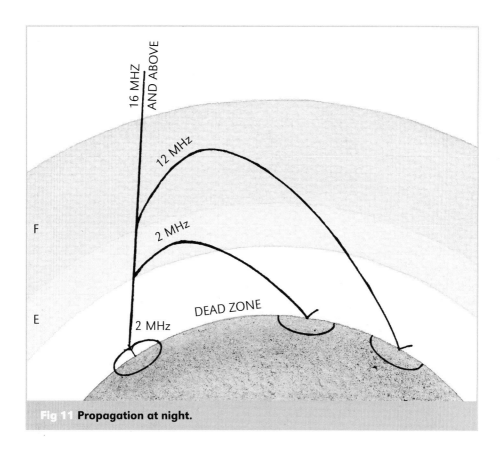

16 MHZ AND ABOVE

12 MHz

2 MHz

F

E

2 MHz

DEAD ZONE

Fig 11 **Propagation at night.**

SKY WAVE

The HF ground wave range is limited to a few miles, so the sky wave is used to enable world-wide communications. Range is dependent on the propagation path rather than transmitter power output. The higher the frequency that can be used, the greater the range as the attenuation (weakening) of the radio wave is less and the skip distance is greater. To work out an appropriate frequency for use, make an estimate, using a propagation prediction chart if available. This will take the path length between the two stations into consideration, along with the daylight/night-time conditions. When using HF, the daylight frequency will be approximately twice the night-time frequency. For example, from the Indian Ocean to the UK, 22 MHz might be used for an all daylight path and 8 MHz for an all night-time path. If the path is a mixture of daytime and night-time, the frequency will be constrained by the night-time path and 12 MHz might be appropriate. At certain times, long distance east to west communications can be limited to a very short window, maybe only a few hours each day. Listen to your estimated frequency; if there is no working, wait for a traffic list or listen to the telex frequency of the coast station, where a continuous transmission of their callsign in Morse will be heard. If reception is good, this band is suitable for radiotelephony communications; if not, try another. The ability to work out propagation paths will improve with practice and is a skill worth achieving. Instead of calling a European coast radio station on VHF requesting an expensive link call to America, an operator could work out the path, call America direct on HF and only pay for a local link call.

To help you to remember

As frequency increases, distance increases.
Frequencies come **D**own in the **D**ark.
Frequencies above 12 MHz are generally not usable at night.

DIRECT WAVE

VHF is said to use a direct wave, producing a line of sight transmission. The ground wave produced by a VHF wave is not usable and the sky wave is not refracted by the ionosphere and returned to earth. At full power, the range of VHF communications is determined only by the height of the two aerials involved. For example, up to 60 nautical miles could be achieved between a ship and a coast station, but only in the region of 15 nautical miles between two yachts and much less between two small fishing boats (see Figure 12). Greater ranges can be achieved between ships and search and rescue aircraft because of their altitude.

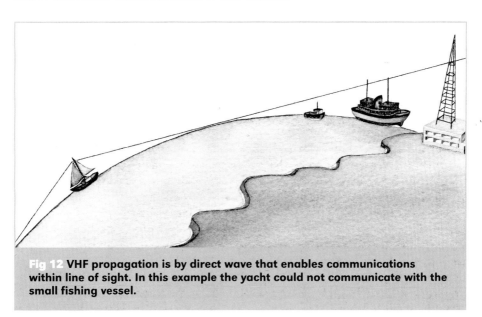

Fig 12 **VHF propagation is by direct wave that enables communications within line of sight. In this example the yacht could not communicate with the small fishing vessel.**

SPACE WAVE

Ultra High Frequency (UHF) uses a direct wave. When used for INMARSAT communications, 1.5/1.6 GHz, it is sometimes referred to as a space wave. This wave is hardly affected by the ionosphere; however, heavy snow or rainfall can adversely affect it.

Practical uses within radio frequency bands

Low Frequency LF 30 to 300 kHz	198 kHz Radio 4 – 'long wave'
Medium Frequency MF 300 kHz to 3 MHz	Medium range maritime communications. Navtex. (Marine MF is 1.6–4 MHz.)
High Frequency HF 3 to 30 MHz	World-wide maritime communications. (Marine HF is 4–27.5 MHz.)
Very High Frequency VHF 30 to 300 MHz	Short range maritime communications. (Marine VHF is 156–174 MHz.)
Ultra High Frequency UHF 300 MHz to 3 GHz	EPIRBs and INMARSAT communications. GPS position fixing system.
Super High Frequency SHF 3 to 30 GHz	Radar and SARTs.

As the frequency increases, the wavelength decreases. Low frequency wavelengths can be in excess of one kilometre, whereas the super high frequency wavelength is only a few centimetres.

To help you to remember

Picture the radio wave entering the ionosphere and colliding with the free electrons and ions. The smaller the wavelength, the smaller the chance of collision. VHF and UHF radio waves can, therefore, escape the ionosphere and be used for satellite communications.

QUESTIONS

1 What do you understand by the mode A3E?

2 What do you understand by the mode H3E?

3 When was H3E used?

4 What do you understand by the mode J3E?

5 What do you understand by the mode R3E?

6 When would R3E be used?

7 What function does the clarifier or fine tune control have?

8 What is a dead zone?

9 Which layers exist in the ionosphere during the day?

10 Which layers can be used in the ionosphere during the night?

11 Which mode of propagation do you associate with MF transmissions?

12 Which mode of propagation do you associate with HF transmissions?

13 Which mode of propagation do you associate with VHF transmissions?

14 Which mode of propagation do you associate with UHF transmissions?

ANSWERS

1 A3E has a full carrier and double sideband.

2 H3E has a full carrier and single sideband.

3 H3E was used on 2182 kHz.

4 J3E has a single sideband with suppressed carrier.

5 R3E has a single sideband with reduced carrier.

6 R3E would only be used if the receiving station requested it.

7 The clarifier or fine tune is used to clarify the received voice by slightly altering the frequency of the carrier reinsertion.

8 A dead zone is the geographical area between the transmitter and returning sky wave where the transmission cannot be received by any station.

9 During the day D, E, F1 and F2 layers exist in the ionosphere.

10 During the night the D layer becomes very weak; however, the E layer and the combined F layers can be used.

11 MF is associated with ground wave propagation. However, at night, sky wave propagation may also be used.

12 HF is associated with sky wave propagation.

13 VHF uses direct wave propagation.

14 UHF uses direct wave propagation that is often called a space wave.

Chapter 4

GENERAL REGULATIONS AND PROCEDURES

The Radio Regulations are agreed at meetings of the World Administrative Radio Council (WARC), which is part of the International Telecommunications Union (ITU), which is itself part of the United Nations (UN). Each country has an administrative body in place to police the regulations by controlling the licensing and operation of ship radio installations. In the United Kingdom, the Maritime and Coastguard Agency (MCA), part of the Department of Transport, is responsible for marine radio matters. The Association of Marine Electronic and Radio Colleges (AMERC) carries out examinations and certification of operators for the ROC, LRC and GOC on behalf of the MCA. The Office of Communications (Ofcom) issues Ship Radio Licences and Maritime Mobile Service Identity (MMSI) numbers. Appropriate authorities can inspect operators' certificates and the radio installation at any time, either at home or abroad. Poor radio equipment found during such inspections may be confiscated. Breach of the radio regulations may result in the authority to operate being suspended or revoked.

The Master, or person responsible for the vessel, has absolute authority over the radio installation. Operators use the radio equipment under the authority of the Master. However, the operators are still responsible for the correct use of the equipment. Unlicensed persons may use the radio installation under the supervision of a licensed operator. It should be noted that Section 11 of the 1884 Post Office Protection Act applies. This Act forbids the reception of communications, other than those for which the station is licensed. If such communications are unwittingly received, they must not be revealed in any way.

IDENTIFICATION OF STATIONS

Every transmission must include the station's identification. Ships at sea and coast stations on land are usually referred to by name. Coast Radio Stations (CRS) are named after the geographical location of the antenna followed by the word 'radio'. For example, Land's End Radio had its antenna situated at Land's End. Coastguard stations are named after the area that they control. For example, Solent Coastguard controls the Solent area.

In addition, if a station operates licensed communications equipment, it will be allocated an international callsign, which is an alphanumeric identifier that is unique to it, similar to the registration number of a car. The first letter identifies the country of registration. The UK allocations are G, M or 2, therefore MLXE8 would belong to a

UK vessel. If a vessel changes hands but stays with the same flag, it will keep its callsign, in the same way that a car would keep its registration number.

Survival craft stations may use the callsign of the parent ship, followed by an extra two digits, which should not be 0 or 1 if immediately following a letter.

The GMDSS has introduced a new type of identification known as the Maritime Mobile Service Identity (MMSI), which is a **nine-digit** identity with no letters. The Maritime Identification Digits (MID) are three digits within the MMSI that identify the country of registration. The UK allocation is 232, 233, 234 and 235. A ship's MMSI is made up of the three-digit MID followed by its own six-digit identity. The coast station MMSI is made up of 00, then the MID, followed by the coast station's four-digit identity. An MMSI used by a group of ships is made up of 0, then the MID, followed by the five-digit group identity. If a ship has a group MMSI, it will also have an individual MMSI.

Example of MMSI numbers

Ship MMSI	123 123456
Coast station MMSI	**00** 123 1234
Group MMSI	**0** 123 12345

Finally, we have the INMARSAT mobile identification numbers. Students should remember the total number of digits and the leading digit for each system.

In practice, the leading digit would usually be followed by the MID and then the ship's identity.

Example of INMARSAT mobile numbers

INMARSAT B	**nine** digits commencing **three**	323572645
INMARSAT C	**nine** digits commencing **four**	423264763
INMARSAT Fleet F77	**nine** digits commencing **seven**	764092849

RADIO WATCH

Since 1st February 1999 there has been no requirement to keep a listening watch on 2182 kHz. All ships now maintain a continuous watch by DSC instead. However, ships will continue to maintain a listening watch on VHF channel 16.

DSC WATCH KEEPING

- Ships in sea area A1 should monitor channel 70.
- Ships in sea area A2 should monitor channel 70, plus 2187.5 kHz.
- Ships in sea areas A3 and A4 should monitor channel 70, 2187.5 kHz, 8414.5 kHz plus at least one other HF distress, urgency and safety frequency.

Ships in sea area A3 that have taken the INMARSAT option are not required to monitor the HF DSC frequencies. Owners of leisure craft who do not wish to join in the GMDSS should continue to keep watch on channel 16 and 2182 kHz for the time being. Some

Ships may have many different communication systems, each having its own identification.

countries, including the UK, have stated that they intend to keep a listening watch for the foreseeable future. Other countries have decided to discontinue the listening watch on 2182 kHz. There is no doubt that all shore stations will discontinue it at some time in the future, at which time leisure craft owners may feel it to be prudent to install GMDSS equipment on board.

TEST TRANSMISSIONS

The operators responsible for testing the radio equipment are listed in Section B of the ship's GMDSS log book. Tests of radio transmitters must last less than 10 seconds, must include the identity of the station, should avoid channel 16 and 2182 kHz, and use low power or an artificial antenna (dummy load) if possible. A test call is a system test that does not require a response from any other station. If there is doubt regarding the ability of the transceiver to function correctly, another station should be involved. Do this by requesting a radio check, which is asking for advice about the strength and quality of the signal. The following tests are important during examinations and in practice:

Every day, the system self test should be carried out on the DSC controller. This does not require signals to be radiated, it just checks the internal circuitry of the unit. Battery voltage should be tested and the battery charged if required. Printers should be checked to ensure an adequate supply of paper.

Each week, the external test should be carried out on the DSC controller. This is a special test call to a coast station on MF or HF, taking the safety priority. There is not usually any operator involvement, as a computer system will recognise the test call format and automatically send back a DSC acknowledgement. There is no automatic test call facility for VHF DSC. This equipment should be tested, if necessary, by sending a routine alert to another station. Reserve sources of energy should be checked. Survival craft VHF radios should be tested on board using a working channel and the reserve primary battery should be in date with an unbroken seal.

Every month, the EPIRB and SARTs should be tested, along with a more thorough check on the ship's antennae and batteries (see Chapters 10 and 11 for more details).

When the tests have been carried out, an entry should be made in the GMDSS log book and the operator who carried out the tests should sign against it. When making such entries, always use UTC for time keeping.

DOCUMENTS

Students should be aware of the documents that are listed below. Pay particular attention to the ALRS, as candidates will be expected to extract information from these during the practical examination. One mistake many students make is in not remembering that if, for example, the coast station receives on 2009 kHz, calling stations must transmit on that frequency in order for the coast station to be able to receive them. Any entry in bold type is the preferred channel or frequency. Quite often there are very small figures next to an entry (remember to take your spectacles), which refer to notes that should always be read before choosing a channel or frequency. The hours of watch keeping are also listed. H24 means a 24-hour watch.

ADMIRALTY LIST OF RADIO SIGNALS (ALRS)

ALRS Volume 1 comes in 2 parts and lists the working arrangements of coast radio stations.

ALRS Volume 2 provides information regarding radio navigational aids, including time signals.

ALRS Volume 3 comes in 2 parts and contains details of radio weather services and navigational warnings.

ALRS Volume 4 lists meteorological observation stations.

ALRS Volume 5 is the GMDSS volume and will be of interest to all students.

ALRS Volume 6 comes in 6 parts and provides information regarding port operations, pilot services, Vessel Traffic Services (VTS) and reporting systems.

INTERNATIONAL TELECOMMUNICATIONS UNION (ITU) PUBLICATIONS

Details of ships can be obtained from the ITU **List of Ship Stations**, soon to be known as the List of Ship Stations and Maritime Mobile Service Identity Assignments. Coast Station information is found in the **List of Coast Stations**, soon to be known as the List of Coast Stations and Special Service Stations.

INTERNATIONAL CODE OF SIGNALS

The International Code of Signals could be used when communicating with an operator who speaks a different language. For example, during communications regarding a medical emergency, 'Mike Golf India' would indicate that 'the patient is suffering from non-corrosive poisoning (no staining and burning of mouth and lips)'.

TRANSMISSIONS IN UK HARBOURS

Each country has its own regulations for the use of radio equipment in its waters. Details can be found in the back of *ALRS Volume 1*. UK regulations permit communications with the nearest coast station, which restricts communications to the use of VHF. Broadcast messages may be received and any port operations or private channels for which the vessel is licensed may be used.

SIMPLEX AND DUPLEX

Simplex is a method of communicating in which either reception or transmission is possible at any one time. A PTT (Press To Talk) switch is used to transmit and when it is released the receiver will operate. Duplex working allows transmission and reception simultaneously, as with the telephone system, but in the case of MF/HF, it must have two separate antennae or, in the case of VHF, it must have a duplex filter system.

A simplex channel is one that uses a single frequency for alternate reception and transmission. When listening to a simplex channel with a VHF radio, you will hear both sides of any communications, providing that both stations are in range.

A duplex channel is one that uses two frequencies, one to transmit and another to receive. Duplex channels are used to communicate from ship to shore. For example, when channel 80 is used, the ship will transmit on 157.025 MHz and in order to hear the transmission, the shore station must receive on that frequency. The shore station transmits its reply on 161.625 MHz and the ship must receive on that frequency. The shore station transceiver is, therefore, programmed with the opposite transmit and receive frequencies to the ship transceiver. When listening to a duplex channel with a VHF radio, only the shore transmissions will be heard and the receiver will be silent during transmissions from other ships. Using the duplex system without being able to transmit and receive simultaneously, as with a yachtsman's VHF radio, is termed semi-duplex.

THE USE OF CHANNELS AND FREQUENCIES IN THE MARITIME BAND

There are special channels and frequencies set aside for distress, urgency and safety. All others are termed working channels and frequencies. We will look primarily at the uses of the VHF channels because this is probably the area that is most familiar to readers.

Channel 16 is for radiotelephony communications relating to distress and urgency. Mariners have to monitor channel 16 and it is, therefore, also used as a routine calling channel. This situation will remain for the foreseeable future.

Channel 70 is for distress, urgency, safety and routine alerting by DSC. *Under no circumstances should this channel be used for radiotelephony communications.*

Channel 67 is for small craft safety, the UK Coastguard's working channel. Although named 'small craft safety', the UK Coastguard also deals with the safety of large ships.

Channel 13 is for bridge to bridge safety of navigation by radiotelephony.

The remainder of the 55 channels are allocated for Intership, Public Correspondence and Port Operation uses.

INTERSHIP CHANNELS

Intership channels must be simplex to enable ships to communicate with each other. Channel 06 is the primary intership channel and 08 the secondary preference. Channels 72 and 77 are used solely for ship to ship communications, making them safe channels to use with no risk of interference to coast stations. If you know that the station with which you wish to communicate is close, try low power first. If you get no response, wait the required time of two minutes and try again on high power.

There will be dedicated intership frequencies in the MF and HF bands. These frequencies will be issued with the ship radio licence.

PUBLIC CORRESPONDENCE CHANNELS

Public correspondence channels must be duplex in order to link mariners at sea into the telephone network on land. Most coast radio stations should be called on VHF using full power on their working channels, some of which are computer controlled. However, stations calling on MF can often call on 2182 kHz. Details of working arrangements of coast radio stations can be found in ALRS Volume 1, which should always be consulted prior to calling.

PORT OPERATION CHANNELS

Port operation channels can be either simplex or duplex. Port operations concerning large craft are usually conducted on simplex channels. UK marinas often operate on channel 80, which is a duplex channel. Remember that when other vessels are transmitting on a duplex channel, receivers on board listening vessels will be silent and only the response from the marina will be heard. Because marinas often work the same channel, small craft should call them on low power when they are at close range. If high power is selected, several marinas could hear the call. Southampton VTS operates on channel 12. It is a simplex channel, which is important since all ships should hear transmissions from both ship and shore. Port operation stations deal with the safety of vessels and persons in and out of port and should be called direct on their working channels, details of which can be found in ALRS Volume 6.

CHANNELS 15 AND 17

Channels 15 and 17 should only be available at low power due to their close proximity to channel 16 and may be used for on board communications. It is important to use correct procedure for all transmissions: the vessel's name and 'control' for the Master and the vessel's name and one of the phonetics for each of the substations. For example:

SARPEDON CONTROL
THIS IS
SARPEDON ALPHA
OVER

It is important that this procedure is not abbreviated. It was once common practice to transmit, for example, 'Fo'c'sle this is bridge, drop anchors'. Since the vessel is not identified, a potentially dangerous situation could occur if the wrong vessel's anchors were released.

TRANSCEIVER FUNCTIONS

A transceiver is a piece of equipment that is capable of both transmitting and receiving. A VHF radio will be in receiving mode unless it is transmitting. To activate the transmitter and disable the receiver, the PTT switch on the microphone must be held in.

VOLUME

The volume control on a VHF transceiver is sometimes called the **Audio Frequency (AF) gain control** on an MF/HF transceiver. They control the level of sound that comes from the speaker but they have no effect on transmissions.

POWER OUTPUT

The transmitter power output will be either 1 or 25 watts on a VHF transceiver. Greater power will give a better signal level at range. Capture effect means that the strongest signal will be received by a VHF transceiver, to the exclusion of all other signals. Always use the minimum power necessary to effect communication unless in distress, when high power should always be selected.

SQUELCH

A VHF marine transceiver generates a high level of noise in its receiver circuits. The squelch control is a function of the receiver that suppresses this noise. Adjusting the squelch control as far as possible into the noise will make the receiver as sensitive as possible. There is a school of thought that says this should be done when a distress call is sent so that it is possible to receive responses from the edge of the station's range. However, for routine work an operator would not choose to listen to the noise continually. The control should, therefore, be adjusted back until the noise just stops, for optimum reception. Adjusting the control well past the noise threshold will result in the loss of weak signals. Some radios will have an automatic squelch control.

DUAL WATCH

Dual watch enables the unit to monitor two channels at the same time – usually, channel 16, which takes priority, plus one other of the operator's choice. Again, this is a function of the receiver and the dual watch should always be deselected before transmission. If the dual watch is left on and the PTT switch is depressed, some radios will transmit on channel 16 and some will transmit on the chosen channel.

CHANNEL 16

The channel 16 button, which is often red or blue, may be used in distress situations. This will turn the dual watch or scan function off and should, ideally, give high power for distress working. However, beware, if the low power is selected and the channel 16 button activated, many older radios will stay in low power.

SCAN AND DIMMER CONTROLS

The scan control will scan all available channels. The dimmer control is used to reduce the brightness of the display, or turn the light on and off.

MF/HF TRANSCEIVERS

The remaining functions are associated with the MF/HF transceiver.

The **Radio Frequency (RF) gain control**, sometimes called the **sensitivity control**, is used to adjust the amplification (strength) of incoming Radio Frequency signals.

The **Automatic Gain Control (AGC)** automatically increases weak RF signals and reduces strong RF signals, compensates for fading and produces a steady AF output from the speaker.

The **clarifier** or **fine tune** is used to clarify the reception of speech that is distorted. This can be due to a transmission being slightly off frequency, or by inaccurate carrier reinsertion by the receiver. See page 12.

The **mode control** allows the mode of emission or type of modulation to be selected.

MAXIMUM PERMITTED TRANSMITTER POWER

Always use the minimum power necessary for routine communications, in order to give priority to vessels in distress. In times of distress, all stations involved should always select high power. The maximum permitted transmitter powers on ships using marine radio frequencies are:

25 watts for VHF
400 watts for MF
1500 watts (1.5 kilowatts) for HF

THE PHONETIC ALPHABET

Candidates will need to know the phonetic alphabet for all of the examinations. International callsigns are always spoken using the phonetic alphabet. When spelling words, always speak the procedural words 'I spell' before commencing.

Alpha	**B**ravo	**C**harlie	**D**elta	**E**cho	**F**oxtrot
Golf	**H**otel	**I**ndia	**J**uliet	**K**ilo	**L**ima
Mike	**N**ovember	**O**scar	**P**apa	**Q**uebec	**R**omeo
Sierra	**T**ango	**U**niform	**V**ictor	**W**hiskey	**X**-Ray
Yankee	**Z**ulu				

CONTROL OF COMMUNICATIONS

When routine communications are in progress between ship and shore, the shore station is in control, regardless of who made the initial call. In the case of routine ship to ship communications, it is the called ship that controls.

To help you to remember

If you are in the bath and the phone rings, it is up to you whether you answer it or stay where you are! You are in control, and the same is true at sea.

MAKING A ROUTINE CALL

The first thing to do is listen, to ensure that your transmissions will not interfere with communications that are already in progress. If calling on Channel 16 or on 2182 kHz, the call should last less than one minute and no routine messages should be passed. The call is made observing the following regulations:

NAME OF THE CALLED STATION not more than three times

THIS IS ('delta echo' may be used as an abbreviation for 'this is' at any time)

NAME OF THE CALLING STATION not more than three times

Ending with the word 'OVER'

Once contact has been made, the identifications are only transmitted once. The end of working between stations is indicated by the word 'Out'.

Example of a ship to ship call on a busy channel 16

ARGENT ARGENT ARGENT
THIS IS
SARPEDON SARPEDON SARPEDON
CHANNEL 77
OVER

Reply:

SARPEDON THIS IS ARGENT
CHANNEL 77
(Argent is in control and can agree or select another channel)
OUT

On VHF, when conditions are good, the call may be amended to:

NAME OF THE CALLED STATION once
THIS IS
NAME OF THE CALLING STATION twice
OVER

Example of a port operations call on a VHF working channel

SOUTHAMPTON VTS
THIS IS
ORIANA ORIANA
OVER

If there is no response to an initial routine call, the operator should wait two minutes and try again. If there is no response to the second call, wait another two minutes. Further attempts should be made at not less than three-minute intervals.

DIFFICULTY WITH COMMUNICATIONS

If you receive a call and are not certain the call is intended for you, do nothing until the call has been repeated and understood. However, if you receive a call that is definitely intended for you, but you are uncertain of the identity of the calling station, you can reply immediately in the following manner:

STATION CALLING HOPPY
THIS IS HOPPY
GO AHEAD
OVER

QUESTIONS

1 Under whose authority is the on board communications equipment used?

2 Who is responsible for the correct use of the radio installation?

3 How would you recognise:

 a A coast station's MMSI number?

 b A group MMSI number?

4 How would you recognise:

 a An INMARSAT Fleet F77 mobile number?

 b An INMARSAT B mobile number?

 c An INMARSAT C mobile number?

5 What is the maximum duration of a test call?

6 What are the daily tests associated with the radio equipment?

7 What are the weekly tests associated with the radio equipment?

8 What are the monthly tests associated with the radio equipment?

9 What information is contained within the ALRS Volume 1?

10 What information is contained within the ALRS Volume 6?

11 What is the difference between simplex and duplex working?

12 May you use VHF channel 70 for radiotelephony transmissions?

13 What is the function of the squelch control?

14 What is a more common name for the AF gain control?

15 What is the function of the RF gain control?

16 What is the function of the AGC?

17   What is the maximum permitted power output of:
  a A VHF transmitter?
  b An MF transmitter?
  c An HF transmitter?
18   Which station controls during routine ship to ship communications?
19   State the procedure for routine calling on VHF when conditions are good.
20   What is the procedure that you should follow if you hear a call but are uncertain the call is for you?
21   What is the procedure that you should follow if you hear a call that is intended for you, but are unsure of the identification of the calling station?

ANSWERS

1 The communications equipment is used under the authority of the Master.

2 The licensed operator is responsible for the correct use of the radio installation.

3 **a** A coast station's MMSI would be nine digits commencing 00.

b A group MMSI would be nine digits commencing 0.

4 **a** An INMARSAT Fleet F77 mobile number would be nine digits commencing with a seven.

b An INMARSAT B mobile number would be nine digits commencing with a three.

c An INMARSAT C mobile number would be nine digits commencing with a four.

5 The maximum duration of a test call is 10 seconds.

6 Every day the internal system self test should be carried out on the DSC controller. Battery voltage should be tested and the battery charged if required. Printers should be checked to ensure an adequate supply of paper.

7 Every week the MF/HF external test should be carried out on the DSC controller. There is no automatic test call facility for VHF DSC. Reserve sources of energy should be checked and survival craft VHF radios should be tested on board, using a working channel.

8 Every month the EPIRB and SARTs should be tested, along with a more thorough check on the ship's batteries and antennae.

9 ALRS Volume 1 contains details of the working arrangements of coast radio stations.

10 ALRS Volume 6 contains information regarding port operations.

11 Simplex working uses a single frequency and requires the PTT to be pressed in order to transmit and released in order to receive. Duplex working uses two frequencies, one to transmit and the other to receive. Full duplex working permits simultaneous transmission and reception.

12 It is very important not to use channel 70 for radiotelephony because it is the DSC channel.

13 The squelch control is used to reduce background noise to an acceptable level.

14 The AF gain control alters the strength of the audio frequency and is more commonly referred to as the volume control.

15 The RF gain control alters the amplification (strength) of the incoming radio frequency signals.

16 The automatic gain control automatically increases weak RF signals and reduces strong RF signals, compensates for fading and produces a steady AF output from the speaker.

17 The maximum transmitter power output is
  a 25 watts for VHF
  b 400 watts for MF
  c 1500 watts for HF.

18 In ship to ship communications, the called vessel controls.

19 On VHF when conditions are good the call should be:
  Name of called station once, this is, name of calling station twice, over.

20 If you hear a call but are uncertain that the call is for you, you should do nothing until the call has been repeated and understood.

21 If you hear a call which is intended for you but are unsure of the identification of the calling station, you should reply immediately:
  Station calling ship name, this is ship name, go ahead, over.

Chapter 5

DIGITAL SELECTIVE CALLING

In the early 1980s, the original concept of the GMDSS was built around satellite communications and did not include Digital Selective Calling (DSC). However, DSC now plays a large part and has helped to make the GMDSS as a whole far superior to expectations.

The DSC alert replicates the 'call' in the old procedures. It is simply a way of attracting attention without the need for a physical listening watch to be kept. It is a similar concept to a paging device. The digital signal is very stable and range is slightly increased. This is because it is less affected by certain types of noise, the bandwidth is narrow and there is no squelch control within the VHF DSC receiver. Once a station has been contacted using DSC, radiotelephony communications follow in exactly the same way as they would have done in the past.

The DSC controller is programmed with the ship's MMSI and needs an input of the ship's position. If the ship has a position fixing system installed, it must be interfaced with the DSC, to keep it constantly updated. If the GPS fails, the position may be entered manually, in which case it should be updated at least every four hours, along with the time that the position was valid. The DSC unit now knows who it is and where it is, enabling a distress alert to be sent very quickly if necessary.

Quite often, but not always, the VHF DSC controller is a separate installation from the MF/HF DSC controller. These controllers do exactly as their name suggests, they control the transceivers. The VHF DSC controller has an independent dedicated receiver that will monitor channel 70 continuously but will only be able to transmit through the VHF transceiver (see Figure 13). Units are now being manufactured as a

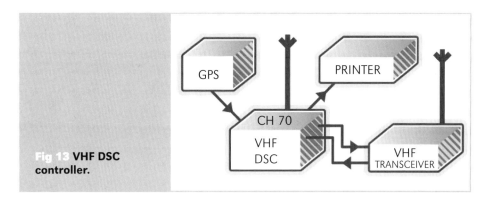

Fig 13 VHF DSC controller.

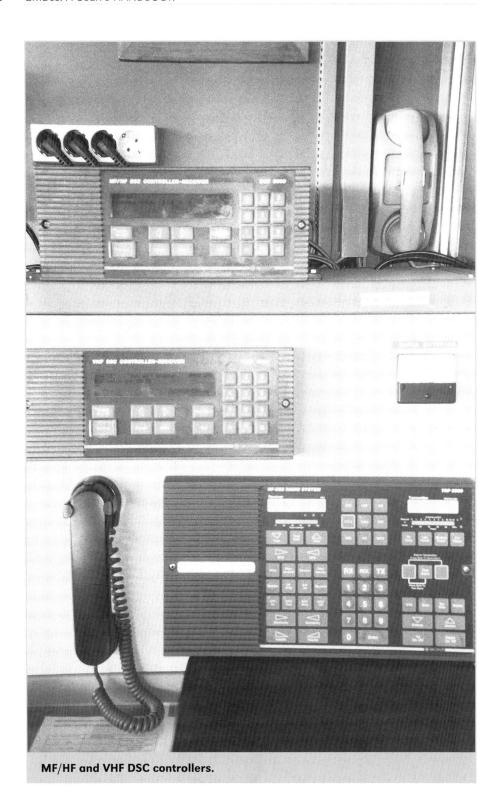

MF/HF and VHF DSC controllers.

combined DSC/transceiver, but it should not be forgotten that there are still two distinct functions to the equipment.

The MF/HF DSC controller has a scanning receiver that can monitor more than one distress frequency. There is a dedicated DSC distress, urgency and safety frequency in each of the 2, 4, 6, 8, 12 and 16 MHz bands. Some models of equipment will scan all six frequencies, others will monitor 2187.5 kHz and 8414.5 kHz plus at least one other HF frequency. It may be possible to monitor one or more additional frequencies, depending on the equipment design – an example could be the MF DSC routine alerting frequency 2177 kHz. The DSC controller will only be able to transmit through the MF/HF transceiver (see Figure 14).

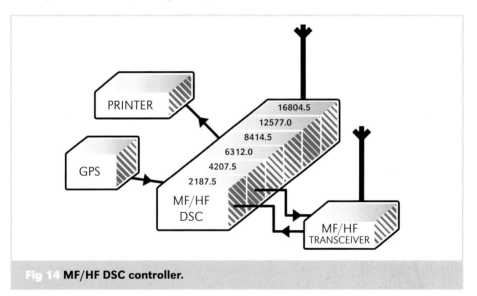

Fig 14 **MF/HF DSC controller.**

DISTRESS ALERT

A distress alert will include a minimum of the ship's MMSI number, the position and the time it was valid. Information regarding subsequent communications may also be included. This will be the appropriate radiotelephony or telex frequency that will be in the same band as the original alert. For example, a DSC distress alert received on 2187.5 kHz will either nominate 2182 kHz for radiotelephony communications or 2174.5 kHz for telex working. Some DSC controllers will automatically tune the transceiver to the nominated working channel or frequency once the alert has been received.

Distress, urgency and safety frequencies used for DSC, radiotelephony and radiotelex. All MF and HF frequencies are in kHz

	VHF	MF	HF	HF	HF	HF	HF
DSC	Ch **70**	**2187.5**	4207.5	6312	**8414.5**	12577	16804.5
RT	Ch **16**	**2182**	4125	6215	**8291**	12290	16420
Telex		2174.5	4177.5	6268	8376.5	12520	16695

These frequencies should be displayed on the bulkhead near the radio installation for practical purposes. However, for the LRC and GOC examinations it is imperative to remember at least those listed in bold.

Two ways of alerting exist – a single-frequency attempt and a multi-frequency attempt. The single-frequency attempt will send an alert on the chosen channel or frequency and wait four minutes for a DSC acknowledgement from a coast station. If no acknowledgement is received, another alert is sent and so on, up to a maximum of five times. If the multi-frequency attempt is selected, alerts will be sent automatically on the MF and each of the HF distress frequencies in turn, re-tuning the aerial each time, without waiting for an acknowledgement. Some DSC controllers will send the alert on 2 MHz first, because this will alert the closest stations, followed by 8 MHz, which is the best all-round first choice for HF. Alerts will then be sent on 4, 6, 12 and 16 MHz in turn. Other DSC controllers will send the alerts in sequential order. Again, it is dependent on the equipment design. In either case, if no acknowledgements are received within four minutes, the cycle will begin again.

The multi-frequency attempt is not the best option to take in most circumstances because one or more stations could receive the alert on each of the frequencies. Each station would then listen to the appropriate radiotelephony or telex frequency in the same band in which they received the alert. The vessel in distress would only work on one frequency, either that on which there is a coast station or the one with the nearest ships. Every other station listening on a different HF frequency would, therefore, hear nothing. After five minutes they would be required to relay the information to a coast station and, before long, half the world would be involved. However, if there are only a few minutes available before the ship's batteries are under water, this is by far the best option to take.

UNDESIGNATED OR DESIGNATED DISTRESS ALERTS

An undesignated distress alert is the quickest type of alert that can be sent. It transmits the minimum amount of information, identity and position, in a matter of seconds. If more time is available, a designated distress alert can be sent giving the nature of the distress selected from a pre-programmed list of designators. These are:

- FIRE OR EXPLOSION
- FLOODING
- COLLISION
- GROUNDING
- LISTING
- SINKING
- DISABLED AND ADRIFT
- ABANDONING SHIP
- PIRACY OR ATTACK
- MAN OVERBOARD

Distress push-buttons have now been introduced to help combat the high number of false alerts that have been generated within the GMDSS. They have spring-loaded

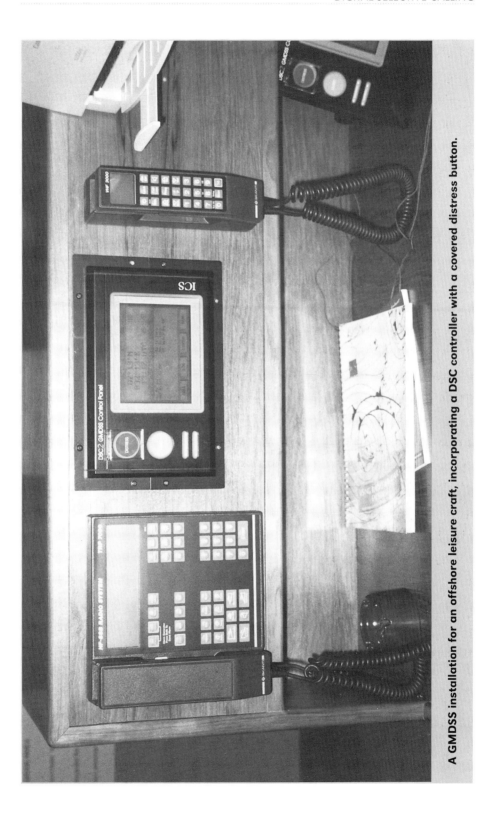

A GMDSS installation for an offshore leisure craft, incorporating a DSC controller with a covered distress button.

covers that require one hand to lift them and a second hand to press and hold the distress button for at least 5 seconds. Two button systems also exist. All distress buttons should have protective covers.

RECEIPT AND ACKNOWLEDGEMENT OF DSC ALERTS

Once a DSC distress alert has been sent by a vessel, the unit will usually sound an alarm to warn the crew that a distress alert has been sent but not acknowledged. In an ideal world, the next thing to happen would be the receipt of a DSC acknowledgement from a coast station. The DSC acknowledgement does two things. First, it causes the DSC controller to sound an alarm, telling the vessel in distress that someone is listening on the appropriate radiotelephony frequency for the distress call and message. Second, it prevents the DSC controller from repeating the alert.

When a ship station receives a DSC alert an alarm will also sound on this unit. The alarm is different for a distress and urgency alert than it is for a routine alert, enabling crew members to tell the difference without having to read the displayed information. Accepting the alert silences this alarm and clears the information to the log, from where it can be retrieved at a later time.

MF OR VHF PROCEDURE

If a vessel receives a distress alert on MF or VHF, the procedure is to:

- COMMENCE LOG KEEPING AND INFORM THE MASTER
- SET WATCH ON THE APPROPRIATE RADIOTELEPHONY OR TELEX FREQUENCY IN THE SAME BAND
- WAIT A SHORT WHILE FOR A COAST STATION TO ACKNOWLEDGE, IF ONE IS IN RANGE
- ACKNOWLEDGE BY RADIOTELEPHONY
- IF NO RESPONSE OR NO WORKING HEARD, THE ALERT REPEATS AND FIVE MINUTES HAVE PASSED ACKNOWLEDGE BY DSC
- RELAY THE INFORMATION ASHORE BY ANY MEANS

It is not the responsibility of a vessel to acknowledge by DSC because this would prevent the DSC controller on the vessel in distress from sending more alerts. The requirement is to involve a coast station in the rescue whenever possible. This is why the first response of a ship should be to acknowledge by radiotelephony. If you were in an area covered by a coast station, you would delay this action for a short time to allow the coast station to answer first, exactly as you did in the past with radio-telephony communications. If you were in area A3 and received the alert on channel 70, you would acknowledge immediately. If you were in area A3 and received the alert on 2187.5 kHz, you would acknowledge immediately if the vessel was close, but if not, delay a short time to allow closer vessels to acknowledge first. If the vessel in distress does not respond to your radiotelephony acknowledgement and the alert repeats, you know that there is no shore involvement and there is little option other than to acknowledge by DSC as a last resort.

If you take this action, you must also take it upon yourself to relay the information ashore by whatever means you have available. To avoid congestion of channel 70 in an A1 area, it is not advisable to acknowledge by DSC, unless the alert repeats every four minutes. The class D controller does not have the facility to acknowledge by DSC because it is designed for use in A1 areas with good coast station coverage.

HF PROCEDURE

If a vessel receives a distress alert on HF, the procedure is:

- COMMENCE LOG KEEPING AND INFORM THE MASTER
- **DO NOT ACKNOWLEDGE**
- SET WATCH ON APPROPRIATE RADIOTELEPHONY OR TELEX FREQUENCY IN THE SAME BAND
- IF NOTHING IS HEARD IN FIVE MINUTES, RELAY ASHORE

The vessel in distress could be half way round the world and you cannot offer any physical assistance. Therefore, you must not acknowledge receipt of an HF DSC alert.

The flow chart in Figure 15 (on page 42) describes the actions a station should take on receiving a DSC distress alert.

DISTRESS ALERT RELAY

Upon receiving a DSC distress alert relay from another ship, follow the same procedure as for the acknowledgement of a distress alert. However, if the relay is from a coast station on HF and addressed to all ships within a geographic area, the ship should acknowledge by radiotelephony on the appropriate frequency in the same band. This is because it is a distress alert relay on HF and the vessel in distress is probably in close proximity.

URGENCY ALERT

Vessels receiving a DSC urgency alert should:

- COMMENCE LOG KEEPING AND INFORM THE MASTER
- SET WATCH ON THE APPROPRIATE CHANNEL OR FREQUENCY
- IF A MESSAGE IS HEARD, RESPOND BY RADIOTELEPHONY IF APPROPRIATE. OTHERWISE, LISTEN FOR FIVE MINUTES
- IF NO MESSAGE OR WORKING IS HEARD, CONTACT AN MRCC OR CS.
- CONTINUE ROUTINE WORKING

SAFETY ALERT

Vessels receiving a DSC safety alert addressed to all ships should not acknowledge receipt but listen to the channel or frequency indicated for the safety message. Again, this is what happened in the past with radiotelephony communications. You would not have acknowledged a call from Niton Radio inviting all ships to listen to the navigational warnings.

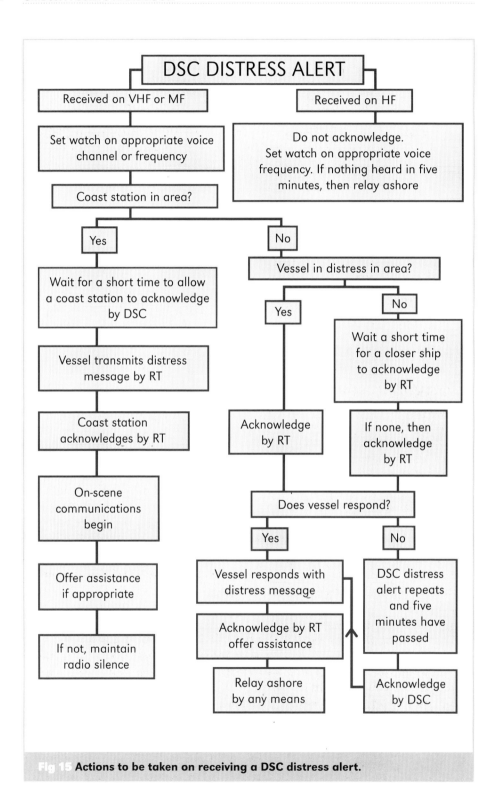

Fig 15 Actions to be taken on receiving a DSC distress alert.

ROUTINE ALERT

If a vessel receives an individual routine alert from another vessel or coast station, a DSC acknowledgement should be transmitted indicating whether the vessel is able to communicate as requested. The receipt of an individual routine DSC alert is the only time a DSC acknowledgement is always sent. If a coast station is unable to accept the ship's traffic immediately it is the responsibility of the ship to make contact later. In ship to ship communications the called ship would make contact at a later time if it was not able to accept traffic immediately.

DSC PRIORITIES

The distress button is only used for 'own ship' distress situations. All priority alerts may, however, be generated via the call button.

The options on a Class A controller are:

- DISTRESS
- DISTRESS RELAY
- ALL SHIPS URGENCY
- ALL SHIPS SAFETY
- INDIVIDUAL
- GROUP
- GEOGRAPHIC AREA
- TELEPHONE

The options on a Class D controller are:

- DISTRESS
- ALL SHIPS URGENCY
- ALL SHIPS SAFETY
- INDIVIDUAL with intership working channel options 06, 08, 72 and 77.

With a Class D controller, the channel 70 receiver is not required to operate when the transmitter is in use. Only one antenna is required. Any alerts that occur whilst the transmitter is in use will not, therefore, be recorded. If an alert is received, then the DSC controller will automatically switch the transceiver to the working channel identified within the incoming alert.

It is important to remember the specific DSC priorities. For instance, if you were asked which priority alert you would send on behalf of another vessel in distress, the answer would be 'distress relay'. Answering 'Mayday relay' would be incorrect because that signal is relevant to radiotelephony communications, not DSC.

Any type of alert that is received by the controller will automatically be stored in the unit's log. The capacity of the log will differ from unit to unit.

CLASSES OF DSC CONTROLLER

Each class of controller will have different functions. The class A controller is the most sophisticated as it will enable geographic area alerts and automatic telephone calls without the intervention of an operator. The class A controller is the type that will most often be installed on compulsorily fitted vessels. The VHF class D controller has been produced for the leisure market. Alerting for own ship distress, urgency and safety is possible, in addition to routine alerting to an individual station or a group of stations.

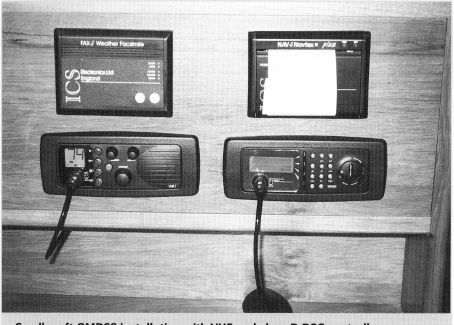

Small craft GMDSS installation with VHF and class D DSC controller.

CANCELLING FALSE ALERTS

If a DSC distress alert is sent in error, it is important to cancel it. The rescue authorities could waste much valuable time and lives could unnecessarily be put at risk if an operator fails to do this. Let the alert finish and stop it from repeating by switching the unit off or pressing the cancel button. Tune the transceiver to the channel or frequency advised in the alert – this may already have been done automatically by the controller. Make a transmission to all stations cancelling the false alert and include your MMSI number. If an operator has been careless enough to send a multi-frequency distress alert in error, he or she is going to be busy as transmissions will have to be made in each band.

An example of a transmission made to cancel a false alert:

ALL STATIONS x 3
THIS IS
NAME x 3
CALLSIGN x 1
MMSI x 1
CANCEL MY DISTRESS ALERT (OF TIME IN UTC)
OUT

AVOIDING FALSE ALERTS

It is far better, for all concerned, to avoid sending false alerts. Ensure that all crew members likely to use the equipment on board have been instructed in its correct use. With modern equipment it is difficult to send an alert in error because of the spring-loaded cover on the distress button and the requirement to hold the button in for five seconds. The older types of equipment were not as well designed and it is easier to send a distress alert in error. Our world has become very automated and many of us have developed a habit of random button pushing in preference to reading the instruction manual. This must not be permitted. If the unit has any complicated functions, display the instructions on the bulkhead if necessary. One of the people nominated in the GMDSS log book should carry out the daily and weekly tests and ensure that false alerts are not generated during the testing procedure. If the ship changes hands, ensure that the registration of the MMSI is updated and, if necessary, that the unit is reprogrammed.

QUESTIONS

1   What is the minimum amount of information that can be included in a DSC distress alert?

2   What is a distress alert called that includes the minimum amount of information?

3   If the nature of the distress is included, what is this type of alert?

4   If you are in an A3 area and receive a DSC distress alert on 2187.5 kHz, what is the procedure that you should follow?

5   If you are in an A1 area and receive a DSC distress alert on channel 70, what is the procedure that you should follow?

6   If you are in an A3 area and receive a DSC distress alert on channel 70, what is the procedure that you should follow?

7   If you receive a DSC distress alert on 8414.5 kHz, what is the procedure that you should follow?

8   If you receive a DSC distress alert relay from a coast station on HF, directed to all ships in a geographic area, what is the procedure that you should follow?

9 If you receive a DSC urgency alert addressed to all ships, what is the procedure that you should follow?

10 Which DSC priority would you select if you had:

    a A distress situation on board your own vessel?

    b A medical emergency on board and needed assistance from nearby ships?

    c A medical emergency on board and needed advice from a doctor?

    d To obtain assistance on behalf of a vessel that was in distress?

    e Sighted a floating container that was a hazard to navigation?

11 What action would you take if you sent a DSC distress alert in error?

ANSWERS

1 The minimum amount of information that can be included in a DSC distress alert is the vessel's MMSI, the position and the time that the position was valid.

2 A DSC distress alert that includes the minimum amount of information is called undesignated.

3 If the nature of the distress is included, the alert is designated.

4 If you are in an A3 area and receive a DSC distress alert on 2187.5 kHz, you should commence log keeping and inform the Master. Set watch on 2182 kHz (or 2174.5 kHz for telex working). Acknowledge by radiotelephony. If there is no response to your radiotelephony acknowledgement, no working is heard, the alert repeats and five minutes have passed, acknowledge by DSC and relay the information ashore by any means.

5 If you are in an A1 area and receive a DSC distress alert on channel 70, you should commence log keeping and inform the Master. Set watch on channel 16. Wait a short time for a coast station to acknowledge. If they do not, acknowledge by radiotelephony. If there is no response to your radiotelephony acknowledgement and no working is heard, relay the information ashore by any means. To avoid congestion of channel 70 in an A1 area, it is not advisable to acknowledge by DSC, unless the alert repeats every four minutes.

6 If you are in an A3 area and receive a DSC distress alert on channel 70, you should commence log keeping and inform the Master. Set watch on channel 16. Acknowledge by radiotelephony immediately. If there is no response to your radiotelephony acknowledgement, no working is heard, the alert repeats and five minutes have passed, acknowledge by DSC and relay the information ashore by any means.

7 If you receive a DSC distress alert on 8414.5 kHz, you should not acknowledge. You should commence log keeping and inform the Master. Set watch on 8291 kHz or the appropriate telex frequency. Listen for five minutes and if no working is heard, relay the information ashore by any means.

8 If you receive a distress alert relay from a coast station on HF addressed to all ships within a geographic area, you should acknowledge by radiotelephony on the appropriate frequency in the same band.

9 If you receive a DSC urgency alert addressed to all ships, you should set watch on the appropriate channel or frequency. If a message is heard, respond by radiotelephony if appropriate, otherwise listen for five minutes and if no message or working is heard, contact an MRCC or CS and continue routine working.

10 **a** Distress alert would be selected for distress situations on board your own vessel.

b All ships urgency would be selected to obtain assistance from nearby vessels.

c Individual urgency would be selected to obtain medical advice from a doctor.

d Distress relay would be selected to obtain assistance on behalf of another vessel that was in distress.

e All ships safety would be selected if you had sighted a floating container.

11 If a DSC distress alert is sent in error, it is important to cancel it. Let the alert finish and stop it from repeating by switching the unit off or pressing the cancel button. Tune the transceiver to the radiotelephony channel or frequency advised in the alert. Make a broadcast to all stations cancelling the false alert and include your MMSI.

Chapter 6

DSC AND RADIOTELEPHONY PROCEDURES

We have seen in Chapter 5 that DSC is a digital automatic alerting system that operates on VHF, MF and HF. The system provides for distress, urgency, safety and routine alerting, the equivalent to Mayday, Pan Pan, Sécurité and routine calling by radiotelephony. The term 'alerting' is used within this text when referring to DSC and the term 'calling' when referring to radiotelephony, purely to help differentiate between the two systems. It is important to be clear in your mind which system you are dealing with. On most DSC equipment however, there is a call button, not an alert button, so do not be confused during practical use when the two words are in fact interchangeable.

DISTRESS

Distress has priority over all other communications. A distress alert should only be sent on the authority of the Master or the Skipper of the vessel when there is serious and imminent danger requiring immediate assistance. A vessel receiving a distress alert should immediately cease all transmissions likely to interfere with distress working and listen. Any vessel receiving a distress signal from another vessel is duty bound to act upon it. This action may be to render assistance or, if another station is handling the situation, to simply keep quiet. The definition of distress has changed with the new regulations to include serious and imminent danger to life. Students should learn that the use of a distress alert indicates that A MOBILE UNIT (SHIP, AIRCRAFT OR OTHER VEHICLE) OR A PERSON IS THREATENED BY GRAVE AND IMMINENT DANGER AND REQUIRES IMMEDIATE ASSISTANCE.

The first action of a vessel in distress is to send a DSC distress alert on an appropriate channel or frequency. In area A1, channel 70 would be used and in area A2, 2187.5 kHz. In areas A3 and A4, 2187.5 kHz would be used to alert nearby shipping and an appropriate HF frequency would be used to alert a coast station if the HF equipment option has been taken; 8414.5 kHz would be a good first choice if there was not enough time to work out propagation paths.

If you have a fast-moving situation, the regulations do allow the transmission of a distress call and message immediately following a distress alert, in order to attract attention from as many ships as possible. However, it is more common to wait for a DSC acknowledgement from a coast station and monitor the appropriate radiotelephony frequency for an acknowledgement from a ship. If the DSC controller is not being updated with position information from GPS, work out a position for the distress message that will shortly follow.

On receipt of one or more acknowledgements, the vessel in distress transmits its distress call and message by radiotelephony. The distress call should be spoken to attract the attention of those craft not yet fitted with DSC equipment.

DISTRESS CALL

The distress call is a broadcast, which means that it is not addressed to any station:

MAYDAY x 3
THIS IS
NAME x 3
CALLSIGN x 1
MMSI x 1

DISTRESS MESSAGE

Without waiting for a response, continue with the distress message:

M   MAYDAY
I   IDENTIFICATION – NAME, CALLSIGN AND MMSI
P   POSITION
N   NATURE OF THE DISTRESS
A   ASSISTANCE REQUIRED
N   NUMBER ON BOARD
O   OTHER INFORMATION
O   OVER

The mnemonic MIPNANOO can be used for distress messages and should be learnt by all students. It may also be used for urgency and safety messages in a slightly modified format:

M   The distress signal is the single word MAYDAY from the French *m'aidez*, meaning 'help me', and should prefix all transmissions during distress working in order to keep the radio silence in force.

I   The vessel's identifications are listed here. Name, callsign and MMSI must be included.

P   The position comes next and is the most important piece of information in the message. It may differ from the DSC position if GPS is not interfaced and the position has been entered manually, and is therefore old. The DSC controller can only display a latitude and longitude. If there is a charted object in sight, use it as a reference in the radiotelephony message because a range and bearing is far more tangible than a latitude and longitude. The bearing must always be from the object of reference out to sea. If using a hand bearing compass to gain a bearing, the reciprocal is calculated by adding 180 to a figure less than 180 or subtracting 180 from a figure greater than 180. For example, the reciprocal bearing of 270°, or due West, is 090° or due East. When speaking these bearings, always use three figures and speak the numbers individually. For example, 5° would be spoken as zero zero five degrees. This way, there is no ambiguity.

N The nature of the distress should be as brief as possible. 'Sinking' is fine, there is no need to transmit the unfortunate circumstances that lead to the situation. Remember that hopefully someone is trying to write your message in his or her log book.

A The type of assistance required will usually just be spoken as 'require immediate assistance'. However, if there is something specific that will help, by all means include it here.

N The number of persons on board is needed to plan the resources that are to be used for the rescue. There is little point in sending a RIB to save 200 crew. In cold waters, where casualties may be suffering from hypothermia, it is wise to advise the numbers in advance.

O Any other information that may assist the rescue should be included. Perhaps the visibility is poor or perhaps there are some distinguishing features that might help identify the vessel.

O The word 'over' indicates the end of your message and invites a reply.

A coast station will hopefully acknowledge the distress message in the following manner:

MAYDAY
IDENTIFICATION OF VESSEL IN DISTRESS x 3
THIS IS
COAST STATION x 3
RECEIVED MAYDAY
OVER

If no coast station has heard the transmission, ships may acknowledge in the same manner, after which the rescue will start to be co-ordinated. Callsigns are always spoken three times when working distress. The procedural words 'Received Mayday' must be in that order, so think 'I have received your Mayday' and you will be correct.

If the above distress procedure is followed and no response is heard, check the equipment to ensure that all of the controls are properly set. For example, if using VHF, ensure that dual watch has been turned off, that the squelch is correctly set, that high power has been selected and that the PTT switch that was depressed for transmission is released for reception. Try again, and if there is no response try another frequency or channel and then any other means that are available to you.

ON-SCENE COMMUNICATIONS

On-scene communications are those between the vessel in distress and other stations assisting in the rescue. On a local scale there are numerous Coastguard stations around the UK that deal with situations daily (see Figure 16). On a wider scale, Maritime Rescue Co-ordination Centres (MRCC) have been put in place specifically to co-ordinate Search And Rescue (SAR) operations. Coast stations (terrestrial), land earth stations (INMARSAT) and local user terminals (COSPAS/SARSAT EPIRB) will all report back via various routes to the MRCC. Simplex radiotelephony is the preferred method of communication, on channel 16 (156.8 MHz) and 2182 kHz. In addition, 3023 kHz and the primary VHF intership channel 06 may also be used for aeronautical SAR. Until informed otherwise, all stations not taking part in the rescue should assist by maintaining radio silence on the frequency handling distress working.

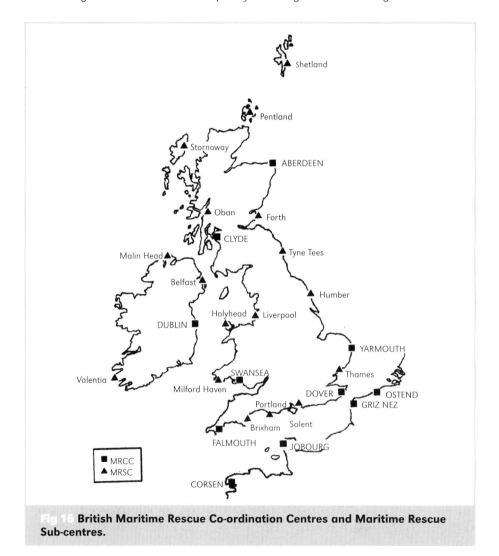

Fig 16 **British Maritime Rescue Co-ordination Centres and Maritime Rescue Sub-centres.**

PROCEDURAL WORDS RELATING TO DISTRESS WORKING

If at any time during distress working the controlling station wishes to impose radio silence on an interfering station, the procedural words 'seelonce mayday' would be used. The controlling station can be a coast station, the vessel in distress, a relay vessel or an on-scene co-ordinator. The words may be included as part of the following transmission:

MAYDAY
ALL STATIONS x 3
THIS IS
NAME x 3
CALLSIGN x 1
SEELONCE MAYDAY
OUT

The end of distress working is indicated by the words 'seelonce feenee', the silence has finished and normal working may commence. The procedural words may be included as part of the following transmission:

MAYDAY
ALL STATIONS x 3
THIS IS
NAME x 3
CALLSIGN x 1
TIME OF HANDING IN MESSAGE
NAME CALLSIGN MMSI OF THE VESSEL IN DISTRESS
SEELONCE FEENEE
OUT

DISTRESS RELAY

When a station learns that another vessel is in distress it may transmit a distress relay alert on its behalf, if:

- Having received a distress alert, it is not acknowledged by a coast station or another vessel within five minutes.
- The vessel in distress cannot transmit the distress alert itself.
- The master of a vessel not itself in distress, or an MRCC, considers that further assistance is required.

It is imperative to make it clear that it is not your vessel that is in distress but that you are the relay vessel. This option is selected from the list of priorities in the DSC controller. In the first instance, a DSC distress relay alert should preferably be addressed to a coast station. The coast station will then appoint somebody as on-scene co-ordinator, if it cannot perform the role itself. The co-ordinator would then send the DSC distress relay alert to all ships in the area.

If a DSC distress alert is received from a ship, a DSC distress alert relay should not be sent to all ships, unless it is clear that nobody else received it.

Next the distress relay call and message will be transmitted. The call must be addressed either to an individual coast station or to all stations. This would match the DSC alert that was sent previously.

MAYDAY RELAY CALL

MAYDAY RELAY x 3
COAST STATION x 3 **OR** ALL STATIONS x 3
THIS IS
NAME of relay station x 3
CALLSIGN of relay station x 1
MMSI of relay station x 1

MAYDAY RELAY MESSAGE

Without waiting for a response, continue with the mayday relay message:

M MAYDAY
I IDENTIFICATION – NAME, CALLSIGN AND MMSI of vessel in distress, if unknown use UNIDENTIFIED (TYPE OF VESSEL)
P POSITION
N NATURE OF THE DISTRESS
A ASSISTANCE REQUIRED
N NUMBER ON BOARD
O OTHER INFORMATION
O OVER

URGENCY

Urgency takes priority over all communications other than distress. An urgency alert should only be sent on the authority of the Master or the Skipper of the vessel. Students should know that the urgency signal indicates that A VERY URGENT MESSAGE CONCERNING THE SAFETY OF A MOBILE UNIT OR A PERSON is to follow. The urgency signal is PAN PAN from the French *une panne*, which means a breakdown. The signal may prefix urgent situations, including a breakdown, the report of a vessel that is overdue, or a medical problem.

The first action is to send a DSC urgency alert on an appropriate channel or frequency. Frequencies used for urgency are the same as those used for distress. The DSC urgency alert may be addressed to all ships, a geographic area, a group of ships or an individual station. Wait for a DSC acknowledgement from a coast station. Ships do not have the facility to acknowledge by DSC. Next, GMDSS regulations require the vessel to transmit the urgency call and message by radiotelephony. The call should be spoken to attract the attention of those craft not yet fitted with DSC equipment. The call must be addressed to either an individual station or to all stations, since it is not a broadcast.

URGENCY CALL
PAN PAN x 3
ALL STATIONS x 3 **OR** INDIVIDUAL STATION x 3
THIS IS
NAME x 3
CALLSIGN x 1
MMSI x 1

URGENCY MESSAGE
Without waiting for a response, continue with the urgency message:

P	PAN PAN
I	IDENTIFICATION – NAME, CALLSIGN AND MMSI
P	POSITION
N	NATURE OF THE URGENCY
A	ASSISTANCE REQUIRED
	(Require urgent assistance is used if nothing specific is required)
N	NUMBER ON BOARD (May or may not be relevant)
O	OTHER INFORMATION
O	OVER

SAFETY

Safety takes priority over all communications other than distress and urgency. The safety signal is SÉCURITÉ from the French *la sécurité*, meaning 'the safety'. Its use indicates that THE CALLING STATION HAS AN IMPORTANT NAVIGATIONAL OR METEOROLOGICAL WARNING TO TRANSMIT.

The first action is to send a DSC safety alert on an appropriate channel or frequency. The frequencies are the same as those used for distress and urgency. The DSC safety alert may be addressed to all ships, a geographic area, a group of ships or an individual ship. The safety call will be transmitted on channel 16 or 2182 kHz. The safety message will follow on a working channel or frequency as it has in the past.

GMDSS regulations require the station to follow the alert with the safety call and message by radiotelephony. The call should be spoken to attract the attention of those craft not yet fitted with DSC equipment. Remember that the call should be addressed to either an individual station or, more often, to all stations and include the channel or frequency for the message.

SAFETY CALL
SÉCURITÉ x 3
ALL STATIONS x 3
THIS IS
NAME x 3
CALLSIGN x 1
MMSI x 1
LISTEN CHANNEL 13 FOR MY NAVIGATION WARNING
OUT

SAFETY MESSAGE WILL FOLLOW ON THE WORKING CHANNEL OR FREQUENCY, WHERE THE CALL WILL ALSO BE REPEATED.
SÉCURITÉ x 3
ALL STATIONS x 3
THIS IS
NAME x 3
CALLSIGN x 1
MMSI x 1

Without waiting for a response, continue with the safety message:

S   SÉCURITÉ
I   IDENTIFICATION – NAME, CALLSIGN AND MMSI
P   POSITION
N   NATURE OF THE SAFETY MESSAGE
A   ADVICE
O   OTHER INFORMATION
O   OUT

ROUTINE PROCEDURES

VHF channel 70 is used for distress, urgency, safety and routine alerting by DSC. Separate alerting frequencies are used for public correspondence in the MF and HF bands – details can be found in ALRS Volume 1. The international MF DSC frequency for public correspondence may be used between ships and coast stations of different nationality: the ship transmits to the coast station on 2189.5 kHz; the coast station transmits to the ship on 2177 kHz. The frequency 2177 kHz is also used for DSC routine alerting between ships.

This arrangement can be confusing. However, if 2177 kHz is monitored, the station will receive routine alerts from other ships as well as alerts from coast stations. If no acknowledgement is received in five minutes, the alert may be repeated. Further attempts should be transmitted at 15-minute intervals.

Details of calling arrangements for coast radio stations will be found in ALRS Volume 1. Ports and marinas have always been called direct on working channels and little is expected to change. If large ports decide to monitor for DSC alerts, details will be found in ALRS Volume 6. UK Coastguard stations have been allocated MMSI numbers and have area A1 DSC equipment. Details can be found in ALRS Volume 5. Some UK Coastguard stations will also be monitoring 2187.5 kHz. Skippers of small craft are not required to carry ALRS and will find all relevant information in one of the nautical almanacs.

CONTACTING A VESSEL WHOSE MMSI IS UNKNOWN

If you are about to be run down by a ship, a DSC distress alert could be used. However, the likelihood of the ship identifying itself from this alert is uncertain. If the ship is further off and you think that a risk of collision exists, a DSC urgency alert could be used. If you know the name of the ship, a radiotelephony call on channel 16 could help you make contact.

A GMDSS console, in the background (centre), as seen on the bridge of a merchant ship.

However, it is never advisable to use radio communications for collision avoidance due to the notoriously poor success rate. It is far better to take early action to avoid these situations.

The main difficulty may come when you wish to contact another vessel for routine communications but you do not know the MMSI number and you do not carry the means to look it up. Routine calling by radiotelephony may be conducted on channel 16 and 2182 kHz until advised otherwise.

Most modern equipment will not permit radiotelephony communications on the dedicated DSC channel or frequencies. However, many transceivers in use were manufactured before the implementation of GMDSS standards. It is important to ensure that radiotelephony is never transmitted on the dedicated DSC channel or frequencies. The DSC receivers will not recognise radiotelephony transmissions and this action could interfere with a digital distress alert.

QUESTIONS

1 Put the following transmissions into their correct order of priority and explain why.
   a A cyclone warning
   b Ship movements
   c To report sighting of red flares
   d A request for medical advice

2 What does the use of the distress priority indicate?

3 If you send a DSC distress alert on channel 70 in an A1 area and receive no DSC acknowledgement, what should you do?

4 Give an example of a distress call on 2182 kHz and state when it would be used.

5 You are in an A1 area. Your vessel's name is Midnight Blue, callsign MRWA3, MMSI 232123456. You have struck a submerged object and are sinking. St Catherine's Light bears 350° from you and you are six miles off. You have six people on board and an EPIRB. State the full GMDSS procedure that you should follow, including the radiotelephony transmission that you should make and the channels that you should use.

6 If you received the above distress transmission, how should you acknowledge it by radiotelephony?

7 Name the channel that can be used for international aeronautical SAR.

8 If a controlling station wishes to impose radio silence on an interfering station during distress working, which procedural words would be used?

9 What is meant by the words seelonce feenee?

10 A light aircraft has ditched just off your port bow. You are in position 51° 44´N 007° 23´W within area A2 and sea conditions are rough. Your vessel's name is White Tiger, callsign GRWQ9, MMSI 232456789. State the procedure that you should follow, including the radiotelephony transmission that you should make and the frequencies that you should use.

11 What does the use of the urgency signal indicate?

12 You are in an A1 area, your vessel's name is Warrior, callsign MJDS4, MMSI 233123457, and you are a 1500 GRT ship. You have lost your propeller and require a tow. You are in a position where Nab Tower bears 340° and you are five miles off. State the full GMDSS procedure that you should follow, including the radiotelephony transmission that you should make and the channels that you should use.

13 What does the use of the safety signal indicate?

14 You are in an A3 area, your vessel's name is Sarpedon, callsign MGME8, MMSI 234234556. You have sighted a floating metal container that is a hazard to navigation in position 47° 34´N 013° 54´W. Shipping in close

proximity needs to be warned to keep a lookout. State the full GMDSS procedure that you should follow, including the radiotelephony transmission that you should make and the channels you should use.

15   Which radiotelephony signal would you associate with the following DSC priority alerts?

   a Distress

   b Distress relay

   c Urgency

   d Safety

16   Which VHF channel would be used to send a routine DSC alert?

17   There is an international DSC frequency for public correspondence that may be used between a ship and a coast station of different nationality. On which frequency would the ship alert the coast station and on which frequency would the coast station reply?

18   What is the MF DSC frequency for routine ship to ship alerts?

ANSWERS

1 The correct order of priority would be:

   c To report sighting of red flares – Distress relay

   d A request for medical advice – Urgency

   a A cyclone warning – Safety

   b Ship movements – Port operations

2 The use of the distress priority indicates that a mobile unit (ship, aircraft or other vehicle) or a person is threatened by grave and imminent danger and requires immediate assistance.

3 If you send a DSC distress alert on channel 70 in an A1 area and receive no DSC acknowledgement after a short while, you should broadcast your distress call and message on channel 16.

4 A distress call on 2182 kHz would be used to prefix a distress message. The call is: Mayday x 3, this is, name x 3, callsign x 1, MMSI x 1.

5 Send a DSC distress alert on channel 70, followed by a radiotelephony call and message on channel 16:

   Mayday x 3
   This is
   Midnight Blue x 3
   MRWA3 x 1
   232123456 x 1

   Mayday
   Midnight Blue, MRWA3, MMSI 232123456
   170° from St Catherine's Light, six miles
   Sinking
   Require immediate assistance
   Six persons on board
   EPIRB activated
   Over

6 The above distress transmission would be acknowledged by radiotelephony on channel 16 in the following way:

   Mayday
   Midnight Blue x 3
   This is
   Identification x 3
   Received mayday
   Over

7   The channel that can be used for international aeronautical SAR is VHF channel 06.

8   If a controlling station wishes to impose radio silence on an interfering station during distress working, seelonce mayday would be used.

9   Seelonce feenee is used to indicate that distress working has finished and normal working may resume.

10   Send a DSC distress relay alert to a shore station on 2 187.5 kHz, followed by the call and message on 2182 kHz.

> Mayday Relay x 3
> Coast Station x 3
> This is
> White Tiger x 3
> GRWQ9 x 1
> 232456789 x 1
>
> Mayday
> Unidentified light aircraft
> 51° 44′N 007° 23′W
> Ditched in sea
> Requires immediate assistance
> Sea conditions are rough
> Over

11   The urgency signal indicates that a very urgent message is to follow concerning the safety of a mobile unit or a person.

12   Send a DSC all ships urgency alert on channel 70, followed by an urgency call and message by radiotelephony on channel 16.

> Pan Pan x 3
> All Stations x 3
> This is
> Warrior x 3
> MJDS4 x 1
> 233123457 x 1
>
> Pan Pan
> Warrior, MJDS4, 233123457
> Nab Tower bears 160°, five miles
> Propeller lost
> Require a tow
> We are a 1500 GRT ship
> Over

13 Use of the safety signal indicates that the calling station has an important navigational or meteorological warning to transmit.

14 Send a DSC all ships safety alert on channel 70, followed by the radiotelephony call on channel 16. The call and message would follow on a working channel.

> Sécurité x 3
> All Stations x 3
> This is
> Sarpedon x 3
> MGME8 x 1
> 234234556 x 1
> Listen channel 13 for my navigation warning
> Out

On channel 13

> Sécurité x 3
> All Stations x 3
> This is
> Sarpedon x 3
> MGME8 x 1
> 234234556 x 1
>
> Sécurité
> Sarpedon, MGME8, 234234556
> 47° 34´N 013° 54´W
> Floating metal container sighted, danger to navigation
> Vessels advised to keep a lookout
> Out

15 The radiotelephony signals associated with the following DSC priority alerts are:
   a Distress – Mayday
   b Distress relay – Mayday relay
   c Urgency – Pan Pan
   d Safety – Sécurité

16 VHF channel 70 would be used to send a routine DSC alert.

17 The ship would send a routine DSC alert to the coast station on 2189.5 kHz. The coast station would reply on 2177 kHz.

18 The MF DSC frequency for routine ship to ship alerts is 2177 kHz.

THE RADIOTELEPHONY EXAMINATION

This chapter is primarily for the ROC, LRC and GOC candidates. However, the radiotelephony procedures that are included are relevant to anyone involved in maritime communications.

Procedures and log-keeping ability are tested during the radiotelephony examination. Marks will be lost for incorrect procedure. For example, the use of incorrect phonetics, acknowledging a distress message with 'Mayday Received' instead of 'Received Mayday' or forgetting to prefix every transmission during distress working with the signal 'Mayday'.

The radio log is a legal document that must be completed correctly. Each time daily, weekly and monthly tests are logged, the operator who conducted the tests must sign his or her name against the entry. When an operator goes on and off radio watch an entry should also be made to that effect with a signature against it. If a mistake is made, simply put a single line through the entry and initial it. Do not leave any blank lines and remember to use UTC for time keeping.

At the start of the examination you will be given a sheet of paper showing details of your vessel and informing you which sea area you are in and whether or not to expect coast station involvement. These details will include the vessel's name, position, callsign and MMSI. The additional information is for use when reporting your vessel's position and ETA (see Figures 17 below and 18, page 64). Blank log pages will also be provided.

Name of ship SARPEDON   Callsign MGME8
Position 19° 51´N 040° 04´W   MMSI 232181956

ADDITIONAL INFORMATION
You are 10 miles from the incident bearing 180° speed 20 knots
ETA 30 minutes

Fig 17 Exercise details for the vessel Sarpedon.

Name of ship ARGENT   Callsign MPLA6
Position 20° 06 ′N 040° 09 ′W   MMSI 233257683

ADDITIONAL INFORMATION
You are 6 miles from the incident bearing 315° speed 8 knots
ETA 45 minutes

Fig 18 Exercise details for the vessel *Argent*.

The easiest way of explaining this exercise is to run a scenario. This example is of distress working. Only two ships will be used as this is enough to demonstrate the procedures. However, in practice, a group of eight students would normally be examined together. The specimen log at the end of the chapter, Figure 20, is from the vessel *Sarpedon*.

When you are told to start, enter details of your vessel at the top of the page. Then enter the date and the time that you would have carried out your daily tests. Log the entry numbered 1 in the sample log – this will include the ship's position, time it was valid and details of the daily checks – and sign your name against it.

Next, the examiner will give you details of a DSC alert which has been received on your bridge (see Figure 19).

DSC DISTRESS ALERT RECEIVED ON 2187.5 kHz

212445089
20° 01 ′N 040° 01 ′W
1030 UTC
SINKING
J3E

Fig 19 Details of the received DSC distress alert.

Log the DSC distress alert as in entry number 2, taking care to copy down the vessel's position accurately. If either of the distress positions is wrong, you automatically fail this examination. The alert gives a position and time. Remember that this is the time that the position was valid and not necessarily the time that you received the alert. Use the clock for that information eg 1100 UTC. If the GPS has failed, the position could have been entered manually and be old, as in this example. CQ may be used as an abbreviation for 'all stations' in log keeping.

Until the DSC distress alert was received, your DSC controller was keeping watch for you on the distress frequencies while you went about your normal business. You should now sign yourself on watch on 2182 kHz. This is the entry numbered 3 in the sample log.

Entry number 4 in this example is the distress call and message. The call is logged by an entry in the 'to' and 'from' columns; the message is logged in full in the 'summary of communications' column.

The transmission from the vessel in distress would be as follows:

MAYDAY, MAYDAY, MAYDAY
THIS IS
MARTHA, MARTHA, MARTHA,
CALLSIGN DELTA HOTEL ALPHA LIMA
MMSI TWO ONE TWO FOUR FOUR FIVE
ZERO EIGHT NINE

MAYDAY
MARTHA (often spelt phonetically)
CALLSIGN DELTA HOTEL ALPHA LIMA
MMSI TWO ONE TWO FOUR FOUR FIVE
ZERO EIGHT NINE
IN POSITION TWO ZERO DEGREES ZERO
TWO MINUTES NORTH ZERO FOUR ZERO
DEGREES ZERO FIVE MINUTES WEST
I SAY AGAIN MY POSITION
TWO ZERO DEGREES ZERO TWO
MINUTES NORTH ZERO FOUR ZERO
DEGREES ZERO FIVE MINUTES WEST
SINKING
REQUIRE IMMEDIATE ASSISTANCE
ONE FIVE PERSONS ON BOARD
THREE ZERO ZERO METRES VISIBILITY
OVER

Each vessel in turn will then acknowledge the distress message by radiotelephony, following the appropriate procedure. Each transmission should start with the signal 'Mayday' and callsigns are repeated three times. After each acknowledgement in this example, the vessel in distress indicates that the transmission has been received. To make log keeping easier, log both transmissions on the same line. This is entry number 5. R Mayday may be used as an abbreviation for 'received mayday' and SB as an abbreviation for 'stand by', indicating the response from the vessel in distress:

MAYDAY
DELTA HOTEL ALPHA LIMA
DELTA HOTEL ALPHA LIMA
DELTA HOTEL ALPHA LIMA
THIS IS

MIKE GOLF MIKE ECHO EIGHT
MIKE GOLF MIKE ECHO EIGHT
MIKE GOLF MIKE ECHO EIGHT
VESSEL'S NAME SARPEDON, I SPELL, SIERRA ALPHA ROMEO PAPA
ECHO DELTA OSCAR NOVEMBER
RECEIVED MAYDAY
OVER

The vessel in distress replies:

> MAYDAY
> MIKE GOLF MIKE ECHO EIGHT
> MIKE GOLF MIKE ECHO EIGHT
> MIKE GOLF MIKE ECHO EIGHT
> THIS IS
> DELTA HOTEL ALPHA LIMA
> DELTA HOTEL ALPHA LIMA
> DELTA HOTEL ALPHA LIMA
> RECEIVED
> STAND BY

MAYDAY
DELTA HOTEL ALPHA LIMA
DELTA HOTEL ALPHA LIMA
DELTA HOTEL ALPHA LIMA
THIS IS
MIKE PAPA LIMA ALPHA SIX
MIKE PAPA LIMA ALPHA SIX
MIKE PAPA LIMA ALPHA SIX
VESSEL'S NAME ARGENT, I SPELL ALPHA ROMEO GOLF ECHO
NOVEMBER TANGO
RECEIVED MAYDAY
OVER

The vessel in distress replies:

> MAYDAY
> MIKE PAPA LIMA ALPHA SIX
> MIKE PAPA LIMA ALPHA SIX
> MIKE PAPA LIMA ALPHA SIX
> THIS IS
> DELTA HOTEL ALPHA LIMA

DELTA HOTEL ALPHA LIMA
DELTA HOTEL ALPHA LIMA
RECEIVED
STAND BY

On completion of all acknowledgements in this example, the vessel in distress will call each vessel in turn requesting its position and ETA. This may be logged as 'Pos?' These entries may also be logged on one line. This is entry number 6. However, you will see that the callsigns have now changed columns as the vessel in distress initiated the communications. When responding, individual figures should be used and the information should be repeated using the procedural words 'I say again'. Do not forget to log your own entry.

MAYDAY
MIKE GOLF MIKE ECHO EIGHT
MIKE GOLF MIKE ECHO EIGHT
MIKE GOLF MIKE ECHO EIGHT
THIS IS
DELTA HOTEL ALPHA LIMA
DELTA HOTEL ALPHA LIMA
DELTA HOTEL ALPHA LIMA
REPORT YOUR POSITION AND ETA
OVER

MAYDAY
DELTA HOTEL ALPHA LIMA
DELTA HOTEL ALPHA LIMA
DELTA HOTEL ALPHA LIMA
THIS IS
MIKE GOLF MIKE ECHO EIGHT
MIKE GOLF MIKE ECHO EIGHT
MIKE GOLF MIKE ECHO EIGHT
MY POSITION ONE ZERO MILES BEARING ONE EIGHT ZERO
DEGREES FROM YOU
SPEED TWO ZERO KNOTS
ETA THREE ZERO MINUTES
I SAY AGAIN
MY POSITION ONE ZERO MILES BEARING ONE EIGHT ZERO
DEGREES FROM YOU
SPEED TWO ZERO KNOTS
ETA THREE ZERO MINUTES
OVER

The vessel in distress replies:

MAYDAY
MIKE GOLF MIKE ECHO EIGHT
MIKE GOLF MIKE ECHO EIGHT
MIKE GOLF MIKE ECHO EIGHT
THIS IS
DELTA HOTEL ALPHA LIMA
DELTA HOTEL ALPHA LIMA
DELTA HOTEL ALPHA LIMA
ALL RECEIVED STAND BY

MAYDAY
MIKE PAPA LIMA ALPHA SIX
MIKE PAPA LIMA ALPHA SIX
MIKE PAPA LIMA ALPHA SIX
THIS IS
DELTA HOTEL ALPHA LIMA
DELTA HOTEL ALPHA LIMA
DELTA HOTEL ALPHA LIMA
REPORT YOUR POSITION AND ETA
OVER

MAYDAY
DELTA HOTEL ALPHA LIMA
DELTA HOTEL ALPHA LIMA
DELTA HOTEL ALPHA LIMA
THIS IS
MIKE PAPA LIMA ALPHA SIX
MIKE PAPA LIMA ALPHA SIX
MIKE PAPA LIMA ALPHA SIX
MY POSITION SIX MILES BEARING THREE ONE
FIVE DEGREES FROM YOU
SPEED EIGHT KNOTS
ETA FOUR FIVE MINUTES
I SAY AGAIN
MY POSITION SIX MILES BEARING THREE ONE
FIVE DEGREES FROM YOU
SPEED EIGHT KNOTS
ETA FOUR FIVE MINUTES
OVER

The vessel in distress replies:

MAYDAY

MIKE PAPA LIMA ALPHA SIX

MIKE PAPA LIMA ALPHA SIX

MIKE PAPA LIMA ALPHA SIX

THIS IS

DELTA HOTEL ALPHA LIMA

DELTA HOTEL ALPHA LIMA

DELTA HOTEL ALPHA LIMA

ALL RECEIVED STAND BY

Once all students have responded, the vessel in distress will no longer require assistance. This will be indicated in the usual way with the transmission of seelonce feenee, which should be logged as in entry number 7:

MAYDAY

ALL STATIONS ALL STATIONS

ALL STATIONS

THIS IS

MARTHA MARTHA MARTHA

CALLSIGN DELTA HOTEL ALPHA LIMA

MMSI TWO ONE TWO FOUR FOUR FIVE

ZERO EIGHT NINE

TIME ONE ONE ONE ZERO UTC

THE VESSEL MARTHA

SEELONCE FEENEE

OUT

The last entry, which is number 8 in this example, is to sign yourself off watch. If it were appropriate, you would also put your batteries on charge at this point.

This is just one example of a radiotelephony scenario in order to demonstrate log keeping in detail. During the examination students may be required to provide the position information without being prompted to do so by the examiner. However, these transmissions have been included in the example because it provides a more realistic concept of how the communications would happen in practice. It is also possible that exercises may revolve around distress relay situations.

Radio Log

Vessel ...SARPEDON... **Callsign** ...M.G.M.E.8.

	Date/Time	To	From	Summary of Communications	Frequency
①	12.09.09 0900 UTC			Position 19°51'N 040°04'W 0900 UTC	
				DSC, batteries & printer tested @ Behand.	
②	1100	CQ	212445089	DSC distress alert 20°01'N 040°01'W	2187.5kHz
③	1101			at 1030 UTC Sinking 33E	2182 kHz
				Set Watch @ Behand.	
④	1103	Mayday	DHAL	Mayday Martha DHAL 212445089 in position 20°02'N 040°05'W Sinking Require immediate assistance 15 POB 300m visibility. Over.	
⑤	1106	DHAL	MGME8	Sarpedon R. Mayday	SB "
	1107	DHAL	MPLAG	Argent R. Mayday	SB "
⑥	1108	MGME8	DHAL	Pos? 10 miles bearing 180° from you, speed 20 kn ETA 30 mins.	SB "
⑦	1109	MPLAG	DHAL	Pos? 6 miles bearing 315° from you, speed 8 kn ETA 45 mins.	SB "
⑧	1110	CQ	DHAL	Mayday 1110 UTC Martha Seelonce Feenee. Off watch @ Behand.	2187.5kHz

Fig 20 Sarpedon's specimen log

Chapter 8

THE INMARSAT SYSTEMS

The ROC course does not cover any of the INMARSAT systems. The LRC course covers the theory of Fleet F77, SAT B and SAT C systems but only practical use of SAT C using telex communications. The GOC course covers the theory of Fleet F77, SAT B and SAT C systems. It also covers the practical use of Fleet F77 using telephone or the SAT B using telephone and telex, as well as SAT C using telex communications.

INMARSAT is a partnership involving over 80 countries. In 1999 it became a Limited Company, owned by all existing signatories. The space segment consists of four satellites in geostationary orbit 22,300 miles (35,700 kilometres) above the equator. Backup satellites are also in orbit and could be brought into use if necessary. Geostationary means that they remain stationary relative to a geographical position on earth beneath them. However, the satellites themselves are anything but stationary as they must orbit the earth at a speed in excess of 6,500 miles (10,500 kilometres) an hour in order to maintain their position. The four satellites are each said to have a footprint, which refers to the position on earth from where the satellite is visible and can therefore be used for communications (see Figure 21 on page 72). The limit of each in a north and south direction is 76°, because of the altitude of the satellite and the fact that the earth curves towards the poles. However, since 5° of elevation are required for successful communications, the workable limits are taken to be 70° north and south. There is a large overlap of footprints in an east-west direction, so it is not unusual to have a choice of two or, in some areas, three satellites.

The satellite footprints are referred to as ocean regions. There are four INMARSAT 3 satellites: the Pacific Ocean Region (POR), the Indian Ocean Region (IOR), the Atlantic Ocean Region East (AORE) and the Atlantic Ocean Region West (AORW). The Satellite Control Centre (SCC) in London controls and maintains the satellites, ensuring amongst other things that they stay on station.

Land Earth Stations (LES) perform a similar job to the coast radio stations in terrestrial communications. They provide a link between a vessel, named a Mobile Earth Station (MES), via a satellite to the telephone network and are capable of handling thousands of calls at any one time. Within all ocean regions, each of the INMARSAT systems B, C and Fleet F77 has a single Network Co-ordination Station (NCS) and a network of LESs, some of which will deal with more than one system. It is the job of the NCS to monitor traffic and allocate free channels to both the MES and LES in order to facilitate communications. The same four satellites are used for all of the INMARSAT systems.

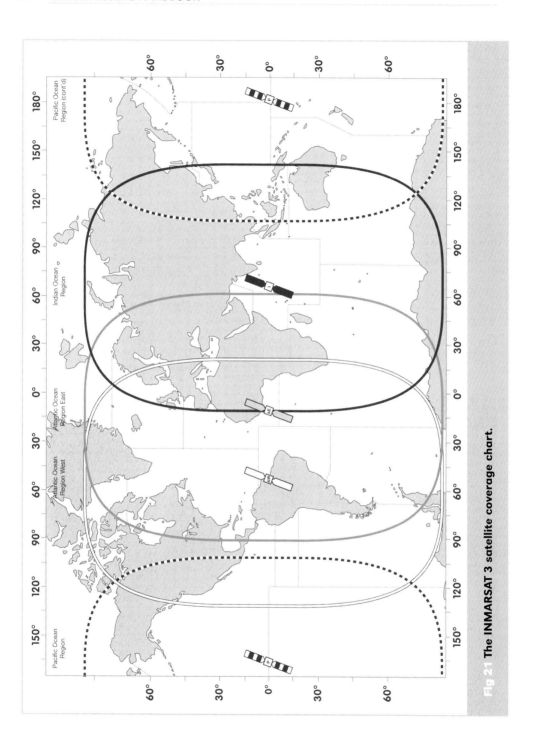

Fig 21 The INMARSAT 3 satellite coverage chart.

INMARSAT B

INMARSAT B was brought on line in 1994. It uses digital technology to support two-way automatic direct dial telephone, telex, fax, e-mail and data transmissions. Digital technology provides high quality and high-speed transmissions with more efficient use of the satellite's resources, which results in enhanced communications and lower charges. This technology can also be used to enable video conferencing.

INMARSAT C

INMARSAT C, introduced in 1991, was developed to provide low-cost digital communications. The system requires a lightweight electronic unit (EU), a PC and a small omnidirectional antenna approximately 20 centimetres (8 inches) in diameter. It meets the requirements for GMDSS and is often the first choice for small leisure craft. It supports prepared telex, fax and data transmissions using a store and forward technique. The system uses Time-Division Multiplexing (TDM), meaning that small packets of information are sent from the SAT C terminal when the satellite channel is free. Up to 22 ships can use the same channel simultaneously but in rotation, with the system accepting a packet of information from each ship in turn. This happens automatically with no action being required by the user. The message is reconstituted at the LES and checked for error before it is sent on to its destination, hence the term 'store and forward'. The technique puts a delay of several minutes into the system, so

Antennae for INMARSAT B systems.

neither voice communications nor live telex are possible. SAT C is particularly useful for receiving Enhanced Group Calling (EGC) services. SafetyNET, used to broadcast MSI, the satellite equivalent to Navtex, is one such service and is free of charge. FleetNET is a subscription service that is used to send confidential information to individual vessels or groups of vessels – for example, race participants could receive specialist weather information.

INMARSAT FLEET F77

Fleet F77, introduced in 2005, brings a new dimension to INMARSAT's portfolio. It features pre-emption and prioritisation, ensuring non-essential communications will be terminated, so that more urgent traffic can be sent. Distress will pre-empt all other communications. Urgency will pre-empt everything other than distress, and so on. This system is also useful for providing Internet and e-mail services.

OPERATIONS

Before communications can commence, the associated antenna must have an unobstructed view of a satellite. SAT B and Fleet F77 use a large steerable antenna producing a pencil beam that must point at one of the satellites. On most systems this can be achieved automatically. Once a signal has been detected, the antenna will lock on to it and track the satellite, unless the ship's heading puts it into a blind arc. For example, if an alteration of course puts the antenna behind a funnel, the line of sight to the satellite will be lost, which is something to bear in mind during distress communications. To find the satellite manually, the operator must know its azimuth and elevation. The azimuth is the bearing to the satellite, through 360° around the horizon. The elevation is the angle of the satellite, up to 90° above the horizon. Tables and charts are published to enable operators to calculate the satellite's azimuth and elevation from a given position on earth. The antenna is driven by servo motors.

In practice there may be a choice of satellites, each offering a range of LESs with differing services. Updated information on services can be obtained through SAT C and from INMARSAT themselves. Heavy users of the system can often negotiate discounted rates and LESs sometimes offer incentives to use them. It is, therefore, worth investigating the options before making a choice. To contact a ship from on shore, the maritime access code +870 is the equivalent to the terrestrial country codes. The original INMARSAT Ocean Region codes were discontinued on 31 December 2008. +870 followed by the vessel's INMARSAT identification number will now reach any INMARSAT terminal anywhere in the world.

SAT C operates slightly differently, using a small omnidirectional antenna that is functional virtually up to the edge of the satellite footprint. With this system the vessel must log in to a satellite. The satellite continually transmits on the common signalling channel, with which the equipment will synchronise during the log-in procedure. Once this is done, the NCS in control of SAT C services through the chosen satellite will automatically route any messages to the vessel. To ensure that messages are not lost and the NCS time is not wasted, it is important to log out before switching the SAT C terminal off. More details will be found in Chapter 9. With some terminals it is possible to log in by scanning for the strongest signal. This is not the best option as the NCS could change as the signal strength varies and SafetyNET messages could be lost. More importantly, you do not want the NCS to change in the middle of distress working, as discussed in Chapter 9. It is always best to tune to a specific NCS and make that the preferred ocean region. Your choice may be influenced by the SafetyNET broadcasts you wish to receive – for example, the AORE satellite transmits Navarea 1 information (see Chapter 12 for more details).

TWO-DIGIT SPECIAL SERVICE CODES

Once connected to an LES, in routine priority, many of them offer several short code services. The special service two-digit code will be followed by + (plus) if working telex and # (hash) if using the telephone. For example, code 32 is available with all systems and will connect to someone who can give medical advice. Code 38 is used for

Antennae for INMARSAT C, on the left.

medical assistance or medical evacuation and 39 for maritime assistance, again available through all systems. The system will route you to a doctor or MRCC in the same country as the LES that you selected. Calls using codes 32, 38 and 39 are free of charge and are only to be used for urgency communications.

Safety code 41 is used to report meteorological observations, 42 to report a navigational hazard and 43 to report a ship's position to AMVER.

DISTRESS PRIORITY CONNECTIONS ON SAT B AND FLEET F77

A distress priority connection ensures instant routing to an MRCC. The process is totally automatic and does not involve a human operator. Operators are made aware of the fact that a distress priority call has passed through their station by the use of alarms. The LES will then provide an automatic priority connection to its local MRCC. The NCS in each region will monitor the progress of such a call and will intervene if any problems are detected. If the call has been addressed to an LES that cannot be worked through the chosen satellite, the NCS will accept the call on its behalf. Any call sent with distress priority is therefore almost certain to succeed. The SAT B and Fleet F77 software is capable of selecting an LES on behalf of the operator, using a pre-programmed default system.

DISTRESS ALERTING ON SAT C

Sat C equipment designed after 1997 will not allow alerts to be sent via the keyboard alone but will require the lifting of a cover to enable the activation of one or two dedicated distress buttons. Operators using SAT C terminals can choose an LES and associated MRCC.

AVOIDING FALSE ALERTS

Do not allow distress priority to be selected unless the vessel has a distress situation to report. If the terminal has any complicated functions, make sure that they are displayed next to the unit for all to see. Ensure that all personnel who use the equipment are either thoroughly trained or closely supervised. The manufacturer's instructions should always be studied carefully before any equipment is used.

CANCELLING FALSE ALERTS

If a false distress alert is sent from a Sat C terminal, it is important to notify the MRCC using a distress priority message via the same satellite and LES. The message should include the ship's name, callsign, INMARSAT C identification number, and the fact that the alert should be cancelled as it was sent in error. It is imperative that any operator who knowingly sends a false alert does not ignore the situation.

SECURITY

In order to prevent the corruption of software used for distress, urgency or safety communications, a dedicated computer is recommended.

QUESTIONS

1 Name the INMARSAT ocean regions.
2 Which system uses a store and forward technique?
3 Which system uses a small omnidirectional antenna?
4 What is meant by a satellite's footprint?
5 Why is it important to log out before switching off a SAT C terminal?
6 Which two-digit code would you use to obtain medical advice over the telephone?
7 What should you do if you send a distress alert in error on INMARSAT C?
8 Who is responsible for allocating channels for telephone calls?

ANSWERS

1 There are four INMARSAT ocean regions. They are the Pacific Ocean Region (POR), the Indian Ocean Region (IOR), the Atlantic Ocean Region East (AORE) and the Atlantic Ocean Region West (AORW).

2 SAT C uses a store and forward technique.

3 SAT C uses a small omnidirectional antenna.

4 Each satellite is said to have a footprint, which refers to the position on earth from where the satellite is visible and can therefore be used for communications.

5 It is important to log out before switching the SAT C terminal off to ensure that messages are not lost and the NCS time is not wasted,

6 To obtain medical advice over the telephone, 32# would be used, once the routine priority connection to the LES was established.

7 If a distress alert is sent in error, it is important to notify the MRCC using a distress priority message via the same satellite and LES. The message should include the ship's name, callsign, INMARSAT identification number and the fact that the alert should be cancelled.

8 The NCS is responsible for allocating channels for telephone calls.

Chapter 9

INMARSAT PROCEDURES

Geostationary satellites have to be at a high altitude in order to provide a large workable footprint. The fact that the signal has to travel in excess of 45,000 miles (72,000 kilometres) between a Mobile Earth Station (MES) and a Land Earth Station (LES) introduces approximately one-quarter of a second time delay into communications. Remember that in times of distress this system will not alert nearby vessels to your situation because it is a point-to-point system. This is similar to dialling 999 from home, where your neighbour does not know that you are in trouble and cannot help you.

INMARSAT B AND FLEET F77

PRIORITY CONNECTIONS

Calling using INMARSAT B or Fleet F77 is achieved by a priority connection through one of the satellites. The priorities are distress (P3), urgency (P2), safety (P1) and routine (P0) on older equipment. New equipment may only offer distress or routine. During the set-up procedure of a SAT B or Fleet F77 terminal, a default LES in each ocean region must be nominated for receipt of distress calls.

DISTRESS PRIORITY CONNECTION BY TELEPHONE
- LIFT THE TELEPHONE HANDSET
- PRESS AND HOLD THE DISTRESS PUSH-BUTTON FOR SIX SECONDS
- PRESS # TO INITIATE THE CALL

If the connection is not successful within 15 seconds, the procedure should be repeated. This is a similar concept to picking up the telephone at home. If you dialled a number and nothing happened within 15 seconds, you would hang up and try again.

DISTRESS PRIORITY CONNECTION BY TELEX (SAT B ONLY)
- PUT TELEX ON LINE
- PRESS AND HOLD THE DISTRESS PUSH-BUTTON FOR SIX SECONDS
- WAIT FOR AN AUTOMATIC CONNECTION TO AN MRCC

Once the connection has been made (the equivalent of the call in radiotelephony procedures) the message should follow. If telephone mode has been chosen, the message is spoken. If telex mode has been chosen, the message can either be prepared in advance and sent once the connection has been made or it can be typed live. In either case, always start with a blank line. The SAT B terminal also has a pre-programmed telex distress message stored in its memory. This is known as a Distress Message Generator (DMG) and may be used instead of preparing the message yourself.

DISTRESS MESSAGE BY TELEPHONE OR TELEX

M   MAYDAY
I   IDENTIFICATION – NAME, CALLSIGN AND SAT NUMBER
P   POSITION
N   NATURE OF THE DISTRESS
A   ASSISTANCE REQUIRED
N   NUMBER ON BOARD
O   OTHER INFORMATION
O   OVER

URGENCY PRIORITY CONNECTION

- SELECT TELEPHONE OR TELEX MODE
- SELECT THE APPROPRIATE LES IDENTIFICATION CODE
- SELECT ROUTINE PRIORITY
- INITIATE THE CALL

Once you have the dial tone (telephone) or the GA+ (telex) from the LES, then the relevant two-digit code may be used: 32 for medical advice, 38 for medical assistance or medical evacuation and 39 for maritime assistance. Remember to add a # for telephone or a + for telex.

URGENCY MESSAGE BY TELEPHONE OR TELEX

P   PAN PAN
I   IDENTIFICATION – NAME, CALLSIGN AND SAT NUMBER
P   POSITION
N   NATURE OF THE URGENCY
A   ASSISTANCE REQUIRED
N   NUMBER ON BOARD (if relevant)
O   OTHER INFORMATION
O   OVER

SAFETY PRIORITY CONNECTION

- SELECT TELEPHONE OR TELEX MODE
- SELECT THE APPROPRIATE LES IDENTIFICATION CODE
- SELECT ROUTINE PRIORITY
- INITIATE THE CALL

Once you have the dial tone (telephone) or the GA+ (telex) from the LES, then the relevant two-digit code may be used: 41 to report a meteorological observation, 42 to report a navigational hazard or 43 to report your ship's position to AMVER. Remember to add a # for telephone or a + for telex.

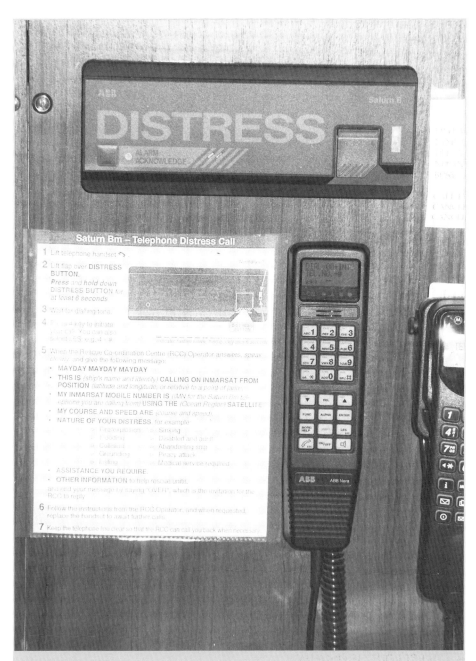

INMARSAT B distress button and telephone handset.

SAFETY MESSAGE BY TELEPHONE OR TELEX

S   SÉCURITÉ
I   IDENTIFICATION – NAME, CALLSIGN AND SAT NUMBER
P   POSITION
N   NATURE OF THE SAFETY MESSAGE
A   ADVICE
O   OUT

ROUTINE PRIORITY CONNECTION

- SELECT TELEPHONE OR TELEX MODE
- SELECT THE APPROPRIATE LES IDENTIFICATION CODE
- SELECT ROUTINE PRIORITY
- INITIATE THE CALL

Once you have the dial tone (telephone) or the GA+ (telex) from the LES, enter:

- 00 for automatic dialling
- COUNTRY CODE or MARITIME ACCESS CODE 870 if calling another vessel
- SUBSCRIBER'S TELEPHONE NUMBER or INMARSAT NUMBER

Remember to add a # for telephone or a + for telex.

When using telex you will receive the shore subscriber's answerback. You should then release your identification by pressing the 'here is' function key, which is often the star key. Next, send the prepared message or type the message live. The subscriber could come back to you before the link is broken. When you have finished, exchange answerbacks using the 'here is' key followed by the 'who are you?' key, which is often the '\' key. If all is well, five full stops will break the connection and, on some systems, give you the duration of the call. However, as always, the manufacturer's instruction manual should be studied with care before the terminal is used.

INMARSAT C

DISTRESS ALERTING

There are two ways of alerting by SAT C:

- UNDESIGNATED – PRESS ONE OR TWO DISTRESS BUTTONS (typically for five seconds)

OR

- DESIGNATED – SELECT DISTRESS ALERT FROM THE MENU, THEN PRESS ONE OR TWO DISTRESS BUTTONS (typically for five seconds)

If no acknowledgement is received within five minutes following either method, repeat the alert. Remember that this is a store and forward system, which accounts for the longer response time. Distress alerts can be sent before the terminal is logged in, and before the equipment is commissioned, so care should always be taken not to send distress alerts in error.

The distress alert sent by pressing the button(s) on the electronic unit will be an undesignated alert giving the ship's identification and last entered position.

If the menu is accessed, more information can be given. Choosing from a list of distress situations can designate the alert. The vessel's position can be updated if this has not been done automatically by GPS. The course and speed can be included in the alert with information taken from the GPS input. Any LES in the ocean region can be chosen. New systems require the button(s) to be pressed to transmit the alert, which will be routed via the LES to its nearest MRCC.

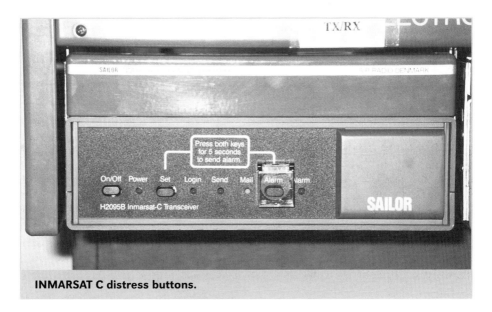

INMARSAT C distress buttons.

It is important at this stage to ensure that the automatic scan facility is set to scan only the ocean region to which the terminal was logged in when the alert was sent. This is achieved by making it the preferred ocean region. If another region is indicated as the preferred one and signal strength increases on the common signalling channel from the NCS of that ocean region, the equipment will retune and communications with the MRCC will be lost.

Whilst the operator is waiting for a response, the distress message should be prepared along the same lines as before with the standard MIPNANOO. The terminal must be logged in to an NCS to send the message.

DISTRESS MESSAGE

Start with a blank line.

M	MAYDAY
I	IDENTIFICATION – NAME, CALLSIGN AND SAT C NUMBER
P	POSITION
N	NATURE OF THE DISTRESS
A	ASSISTANCE REQUIRED
N	NUMBER ON BOARD
O	OTHER INFORMATION
O	OVER (or NNNN because this is sent in store and forward mode)

To transmit the distress message be sure to choose distress priority. This will ensure that you are allocated a distress priority channel through the satellite and will also override any destination information that may have been entered in error. It is important to use the same LES that was used for the alert, so that the message is received by the same MRCC.

OTHER PRIORITY MESSAGES

SAT C transmission priorities are either normal or distress.

Urgency and safety messages have to be sent under normal priority. With this system, the special service two-digit codes will ensure the required priority connection.

To send a prepared routine message, select normal priority. The country code, number and answerback of the destination subscriber are required. If this is a subscriber you contact frequently, the details may be chosen from your destination directory. Select the LES and initiate the call. The message will then be transferred to the electronic unit and sent.

LOGGING OUT

It is important to log out before switching off the IMMARSAT C terminal. Logging out informs the NCS of the ocean region that the terminal is no longer available to accept messages and callers will be informed of this fact. If the operator does not log out, the LES will continue to try to send messages to the vessel and eventually the messages could be lost. Repeated attempts could also prove to be expensive to the subscriber who is trying to call.

QUESTIONS

1   You are in position 31° 24´S 051° 31´W, your vessel's name is Jade, call-sign MENO4, INMARSAT Fleet F77 mobile number 764095687. You have complete engine failure and need to call for assistance by telephone. State the procedure that you should follow and the voice message that you should send.

2   You are in position 01° 13´S 002° 11´E, your course is 090° at a speed of 5 knots. Your vessel's name is Jupiter, callsign GPLO5, INMARSAT B mobile number 323356789,. There are 40 persons on board. You have discovered a fire and need to call for immediate assistance by telex. Two of the crew have been badly burned. State the procedure that you should follow and the message that you should send.

3   You are in position 29° 53´N 031° 32´W. Your vessel's name is Saturn, callsign MRAX9, INMARSAT C mobile number 423334567. You have struck a submerged object and are sinking. There are 25 persons on board and the sea state is rough. State the procedure that you should follow and the message that you should send.

ANSWERS

1   Select telephone mode
Select routine priority
Select LES identification code
Initiate the call according to the manufacturer's instructions
On receiving a dial tone from the LES enter 39# for maritime assistance.

Once connected, speak:
>   Pan Pan
>   Jade MENO4 764095687
>   In position 31° 24´S 051° 31´W
>   Complete engine failure
>   Require urgent assistance
>   Over

2   Put telex on line
Press and hold the distress push-button for six seconds
Wait for an automatic connection to an MRCC

Once answerback is received, either select the message stored in the distress message generator or type the following message, starting with a blank line:

>   Mayday
>   Jupiter GPLO5 323356789
>   In position 01° 13´S 002° 11´E
>   Course 090° speed 5 knots
>   Fire on board
>   Require immediate assistance
>   40 persons on board, two need urgent medical attention
>   Over

3   Either press and hold the distress button(s) on the electronic unit, or select distress alert from the menu and then press and hold the distress button(s). Then type and send the following message, with distress priority, via the same LES, starting with a blank line:

>   Mayday
>   Saturn MRAX9, 423334567
>   In position 29° 53´N 031° 32´W

Sinking

Require immediate assistance

25 persons on board

Sea conditions are rough

Over (or NNNN)

Check that the ocean region that you have used is selected as your preferred ocean region, to prevent change of NCS during distress working.

Chapter 10

EPIRBs AND SARTs

Emergency Position Indicating Radio Beacons (EPIRBs) and Search And Rescue Transponders (SARTs) provide locating and homing signals for use during Search And Rescue (SAR) operations. The EPIRB usually provides a 'ball park' position for the search, with the SART providing the 'fine tune' facility for location of the survivors. If at all possible, keep both with you if you need to abandon your ship.

EPIRBs

GMDSS regulations require the vessel to carry at least two independent means of transmitting a distress alert. The EPIRB provides a secondary method of distress alerting. It relays position and identification information from a casualty in distress to an MRCC. The EPIRB signal indicates that one or more persons are in distress, that they may no longer be on board their vessel and that they may not have receiving facilities.

COSPAS/SARSAT EPIRBs

COSPAS/SARSAT is an international humanitarian Search And Rescue system. These EPIRBs are for use in areas A1, A2, A3 and A4, they operate on 406.025 MHz (usually referred to as 406 MHz) and a 121.5 MHz homing signal is often included. The space segment is operated jointly by Russia (COSPAS – COsmicheskaya Sistyema Poiska Avariynich Sudov, which translates as Space System for the Search of Vessels in Distress) and an American-Canadian-French consortium (SARSAT – Search And Rescue Satellite Aided Tracking). COSPAS is an electronic package on the Russian NADEZHDA navigation satellites and SARSAT is an instrument package on the NOAA weather satellites. There are 34 other participating nations in the programme that provide electronics and ground support. The satellites are able to detect 406 MHz alerts world-wide. 121.5 MHz was phased out on 1st February 2009 and is no longer detected by the satellites.

The system, which came on line in 1982, comprises a number of low altitude satellites in displaced, near polar orbits that are able to scan the entire globe every 2–3 hours. The orbits are set and the earth rotates beneath them. The system is designed to have at least two COSPAS and two SARSAT satellites in operation at all times, although there are often more. Low altitude orbits mean that the transmitter power of a 406 MHz EPIRB needs to be only five watts. The altitude is typically 528 miles (850 kilometres) for the SARSAT satellites, which complete an orbit every

A 406 MHz COSPAS/SARSAT EPIRB in a float-free mounting.

100 minutes, and 620 miles (1000 kilometres) for the COSPAS satellites, which complete an orbit every 105 minutes.

Each satellite carries an SAR processor, which receives and stores 406 MHz alerts. The alert will be retransmitted either immediately if a ground station is in view or as soon as one comes into the footprint.

The satellites communicate with Local User Terminals (LUT) on earth, which pass their information to an MRCC via a Mission Control Centre (MCC). The average notification time is between one and two hours. This is because there is not a continual coverage by the satellites. The delay will be greater at the equator than at the poles. There may be a time delay before the next satellite passes over the beacon and then another time delay for it to be in a suitable position to relay the information to an LUT. One pass is often sufficient for a 406 MHz beacon with a stable signal, although if reception is poor it may require a second pass.

Once an EPIRB is activated, the beacon transmits a digitally encoded distress alert, which includes the identification of the ship. It is, therefore, important to ensure that it is correctly programmed and registered. The alert is received by a satellite and relayed to the nearest LUT. There are 45 LUTs world-wide, which track the satellites using parabolic antennae. They are fully automated and unmanned and consist of computers and communication equipment. The alert is processed to calculate the position of the beacon, which is then routed to the MCC via a network connection. The MCC will decode the identification information contained within the transmission. All of the information is then passed on to an MRCC.

The LUT uses Doppler frequency analysis to calculate the position of the EPIRB, using the motion of the satellite relative to the stationary beacon on the earth's surface. The location accuracy is said to be within 3.1 miles (5 kilometres). However, most location calculations are significantly more accurate than this.

Final location is achieved by a low power 121.5 MHz homing signal that is included in most 406 MHz beacons. 121.5 MHz is the international aeronautical emergency frequency and, whilst not mandatory, it is useful for homing by the SAR aircraft. It is also possible that a passing aircraft will pick up the signal.

Research started in 1987 into the use of geostationary satellites for receiving signals from 406 MHz GPS-encoding beacons. This has been named the GEOSAR system and beacons are now available. Notification time is reduced to a few minutes and position is as accurate as GPS, so these beacons are much more efficient. If the GPS fails, or if the vessel trades above 70° then the standard 406 MHz beacon will continue to work.

ACTIVATION

EPIRBs can be either manually or automatically activated. If the automatic system is chosen, a hydrostatic release is fitted, which will allow the EPIRB to float free when immersed to a depth of approximately 4 metres. Regulations require all compulsorily fitted vessels to install a float-free EPIRB. To help reduce the false alarm rate, most new EPIRBs are being produced with a two-stage activation process. The first action will arm it, for example by removing it from its housing. The second action will activate it, for example by manually switching it on or immersing it in sea water.

SARTs

The purpose of a Search And Rescue Transponder (SART) is to indicate the position of persons or vessels in distress. It operates on 9 GHz, also known as the

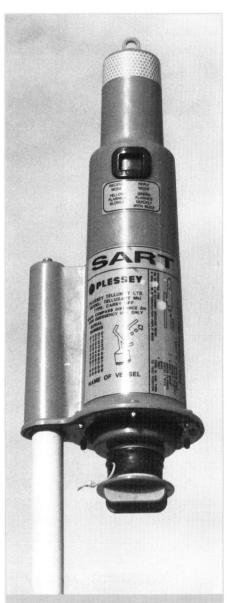

A SART, positioned upright and as high as possible. It should be at least one metre above sea level.

X band or the three centimetre radar band. A transponder is a unit that transmits in response to an incoming signal. A SART will transmit its signals when interrogated by a radar producing a pulse with a wavelength of three centimetres. The transmission is line of sight, so range is unlikely to be more than 10 miles to a ship but it will be much greater, maybe 30 to 40 miles, to a search and rescue aircraft (see Figure 22). Rough

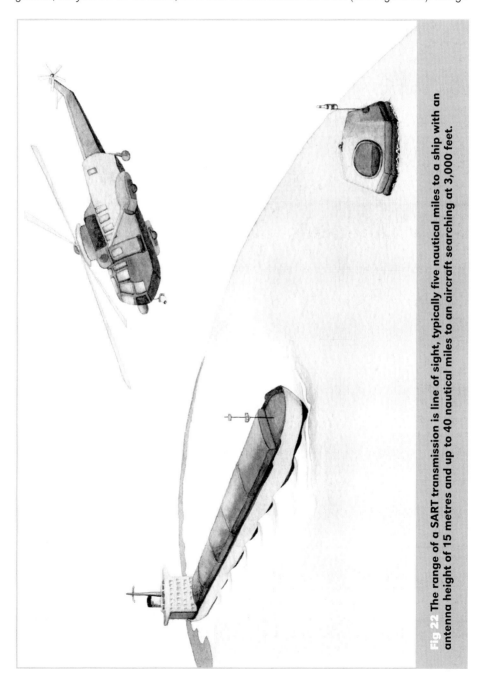

Fig 22 The range of a SART transmission is line of sight, typically five nautical miles to a ship with an antenna height of 15 metres and up to 40 nautical miles to an aircraft searching at 3,000 feet.

conditions will produce a greater range on the crests of waves but loss of signal in the troughs. Flat calm conditions are not ideal as radar pulses can be reflected from the surface of the sea. The SART will sound an alarm and change its light characteristic when interrogated by a vessel close at hand, which is sure to raise morale. When this happens, call on VHF channel 16 and fire flares. The battery should allow for 96 hours in stand-by mode with eight hours of transmitting time. Do not deploy a SART and a radar reflector simultaneously as the reflector may obscure the SART. If the SART is interrogated, it sweeps through the radar frequency band 12 times. When the SART frequency matches that of the interrogating radar during each sweep, it will produce a target on the radar screen.

Twelve dots approximately 0.64 of a nautical mile apart will be shown on the screen (see Figure 23). The dot closest to the ship's position indicates the position of the SART. When the range to the SART closes to about one mile, the dots will change into arcs (see Figure 24). At this point, the position of the casualty is accurate to within 150 metres. As the range closes even further, concentric circles will be seen (see Figure 25). When searching for a SART, choose a radar range between 6 and 12 nautical miles because the 12 dots may extend to nearly 10 miles beyond the position of the SART. If the radar is on a short range and only one or two dots are displayed, they could be confused with other targets.

AIS-SART

From the 1st January 2010, the Automatic Identification System – Search And Rescue Transmitter (AIS-SART) joined the GMDSS, as an alternative to the radar SART.

The AIS-SART is programmed with a nine-digit identification code. The first

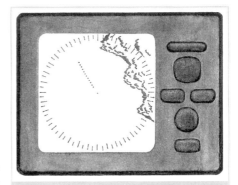

Fig 23 Twelve dots will be shown on the radar screen of a search vessel.

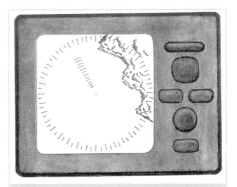

Fig 24 When the range closes to approximately one mile, the dots change into arcs.

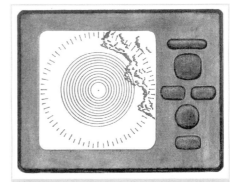

Fig 25 As the range closes further, the arcs change into concentric circles.

three digits being 970, the following two digits are a manufacturer code and the last four a serial number. This is not a unique ID and cannot identify the vessel. It has an internal GPS to enable it to receive position information and battery life is 96 hours.

Once activated, the AIS-SART transmits eight messages, over a 14-second time slot, every minute, on two different channels. One channel operates on 161.975 MHz, the other on 162.025 MHz, and four messages will be sent on each. It is only necessary to receive one of these messages to obtain an accurate location. However, sending multiple messages ensures that this will happen.

Any equipment capable of receiving an AIS signal can also detect an AIS-SART. The identification appears, along with the time, position, range and bearing. It is also displayed on electronic charts as a cross enclosed by a small circle.

The range is line of sight, so comparable to the radar SART. However, there is no AIS receiver, so unlike the radar SART it is unable to inform you that your signal has been received by nearby vessels.

AIS-SART	
ID:	970221234
UTC:	16 : 15 : 30
LAT:	50° 14.450' N
LON:	010° 18.034' W
RANGE:	3.48 nm 184°

TESTING OF EPIRBs AND SARTs

EPIRBs and SARTs must be tested monthly in accordance with the manufacturer's instructions. At this time, also inspect the units for signs of damage or corrosion. Check lanyards, seals, telescopic poles and if it is intended that the unit should float free, ensure that it could do so in an emergency. The batteries and hydrostatic release should be changed if the expiry date is close. Some units will need to be returned to the manufacturer at this time. It has been reported that some 406 MHz EPIRBs pass their internal test but do not transmit if required to do so. It is advisable to have EPIRBs tested annually with a shielded tester that will receive and decode the 406 MHz signal, check the identification and, if appropriate, provide an audible indication that the 121.5 MHz homing signal is functioning.

AVOIDING FALSE ALERTS

During each safety drill, instruction should be given in the use of EPIRBs and SARTs.

It is important to ensure that EPIRBs are properly registered and that registrations are updated if the unit changes hands. Failure to do so can result in heavy penalties. Falmouth Coastguard administers the UK EPIRB register. The EPIRB should not be activated if assistance has been made available by other means. If possible, an EPIRB should be retrieved and deactivated after use. If it is to be scrapped, it should be made inoperable. If it is to be returned for maintenance, it should be either disabled or wrapped in two layers of aluminium foil. Every effort should be made to ensure that the EPIRB does not transmit accidentally. Should this happen, it must be left on until a coast station or MRCC is contacted. The EPIRB will be identified and then you will be asked to switch it off.

QUESTIONS

1   What is the purpose of an EPIRB?

2   What does the EPIRB signal indicate?

3   What is the primary frequency used by a COSPAS/SARSAT EPIRB and in which sea areas may it be used?

4   Which frequency is used for the low power homing signal of an EPIRB?

5   What is the purpose of a SART?

6   On which frequency does a SART operate?

7   To which signal does the SART respond?

8   How would you recognise a SART transmission on a radar screen?

9   How would you know that you were closing on the casualty?

10 How often should the SART and EPIRB be tested?

11 What is involved in testing the EPIRB and the SART?

12 What should you do if your EPIRB is activated in error?

ANSWERS

1 The purpose of an EPIRB is to provide a secondary means of distress alerting as well as identification and position information regarding the casualty.

2 The EPIRB signal indicates that one or more persons are in distress, that they may no longer be on board their vessel and that they may not have receiving facilities.

3 The frequency used by a COSPAS/SARSAT EPIRB is 406 MHz and it may be used in areas A1, A2, A3 and A4.

4 121.5 MHz is used for the low power homing signal of an EPIRB.

5 The purpose of a SART is to indicate the position of persons or vessels in distress by means of a three centimetre radar.

6 A SART operates on 9 GHz, also known as the X band.

7 The SART responds to a signal from a three centimetre radar.

8 A SART transmission appears on a radar screen as 12 dots. The dot closest to the ship's position is the SART.

9 When you close to approximately one mile, the dots start to arc and eventually form concentric circles as the SART's position is approached.

10 The SART and EPIRB must be tested monthly.

11 Carry out the tests in accordance with the manufacturer's instructions. At the same time, inspect the units for signs of damage or corrosion. Check lanyards, seals and telescopic poles and if it is intended that the unit should float free, ensure that it could do so in an emergency. The batteries and hydrostatic release should be changed if the expiry date is close.

12 If your EPIRB is activated in error, it should be left on until a coast station or MRCC is contacted. The EPIRB will be identified and then you will be asked to switch it off.

Chapter 11

ANTENNAE AND BATTERIES

Picture a stone being thrown into a pond on a very still day. Ripples will move out from the position where the stone entered the water. Each wave will increase in diameter and weaken as it moves away from the source. If a duck was sitting on the pond, it would move up and down on each wave as it passed. This is how two antennae react to each other. The transmitting antenna produces oscillating electromagnetic energy at, for example, 150 watts, which travels through free space, becoming weaker with distance. A receiving antenna will receive the energy in perhaps microwatts, which it will then amplify to an appropriate level to be heard at the loud speaker.

VHF ANTENNA

The VHF transceiver is connected to a whip antenna, which can be full, half or quarter the wavelength of channel 16. The thin wire whips that are produced for the leisure market are optimised for 156.8 MHz. All other channels are received as a bonus. You will therefore find that sometimes you can hear two vessels making contact on channel 16. However, when you follow them to their working channel you may only be able to hear one of the vessels. The further away from 156.8 MHz the working channel is, the more likely this is to happen. If you are ever concerned about the strength of your own transmissions, pick the working channel whose frequency is nearest to channel 16.

The full whip antenna is a little less than two metres long, insulated at the bottom and made of wire encapsulated in glassfibre. VHF antennae should be situated as high as possible since the range of VHF communications is determined by the height of the antennae. Since the radio wave is polarised along the axis of the antennae, it is not recommended that it be raked back in 'go faster' fashion. In this orientation, a large proportion of the radiated power will be horizontally polarised and therefore not received by vertical receiving antennae. When using transportable radios try to hold them upright for the same reason. This puts the antenna fairly close to the user's eye. It is therefore not recommended to use a transportable that transmits at more than six watts in order to minimise the health risk.

MF AND HF WHIP ANTENNA

A whip antenna may be used for MF and HF communications. It will vary in length depending on the size of the vessel and type of installation. However, it is often between 7.5 and 9 metres (25 and 30 feet) long and constructed of metal sections

Whip antennae.

encased in glassfibre, which screw together and lock in place. A wire aerial is not aesthetically pleasing. The whip antenna is therefore an alternative and is used on most modern ships. For the antenna to function efficiently, its length must proportionately match the wavelength of the frequency to be used by the transmitter. An antenna tuning unit (ATU), containing capacitors, adjustable coils and a central processing unit, is used to tune the whip over a variable frequency range. This is activated by a tune button on the transceiver. For optimum performance, the ATU should be situated directly beneath the antenna and ideally above decks.

WIRE AERIAL

Wire aerials provide excellent radiation properties on MF. They are usually constructed of strong stranded bronze or copper wire with a ceramic or glass insulator at each end. The insulators prevent the wire halyards from forming part of the aerial. If the radio installation is amidships, a T installation is used and if the installation is aft, an inverted L installation is used. Halyards, which control the aerial, should be made from metal, making them fire proof. Another important part of the construction is the weak link (see Figure 26). This has approximately half the breaking strength of the aerial and provides a controlled breaking point if the aerial comes under too much strain. The weak link is always protected by a safety loop to ensure that the aerial does not fall to the deck and also to maintain its usability.

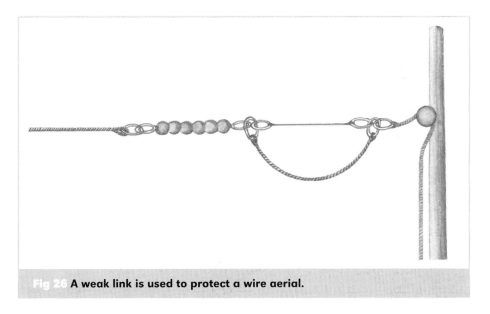

Fig 26 **A weak link is used to protect a wire aerial.**

When the backstay aerial is used on a yacht, it is under a lot of strain and glass insulators are not strong enough. Special non-conducting carbon fibre insulators are used instead.

Antennae used for MF, HF and VHF communications are omnidirectional.

ANTENNAE FOR INMARSAT B AND FLEET F77

These systems both require a large parabolic steerable antenna, which produces a pencil beam. The beam must be aimed to within 5° of the satellite's position. The satellite itself must be at least 5° above the horizon in order to effect reliable communications. Once in auto-tracking mode, the antenna will track the satellite in any sea conditions as long as the ship's heading does not put it into a blind arc. In order to function correctly at all times, the gyro stabilised antenna must have a 360° view of the horizon. Placing of the antenna therefore requires careful consideration. These systems consume large amounts of power and need good control measures to keep them functioning correctly. It should be remembered that in times of distress, when available power may be reduced, the system will only function if the pencil beam is pointing at a satellite, therefore emergency power supplies must be in place.

Both of these systems support speech, so a wide bandwidth is needed and the 50 to 100 watt transmitter output is therefore spread fairly thinly. A dish or parabolic reflector is a means of focusing or concentrating the signal from an omnidirectional antenna into a narrow pencil beam. An example of an omnidirectional light is a bare light bulb hanging from a light fitting. If the same bulb was fitted into a large torch with a reflector, the resulting beam would be focused, stronger and brighter. The same is true of the resulting radio wave reaching the satellite – it appears to have come from a much more powerful transmitting source. The bigger the dish, the narrower the resulting beam and the stronger the signal.

SAT B antennae are approximately 125 centimetres (49 inches) in diameter, 135 centimetres (53 inches) high and weigh approximately 100 kilograms (220 pounds). Fleet F77 antennae are approximately 84 centimetres (33 inches) in diameter, 88 centimetres (35 inches) high and weigh approximately 27 kilograms (60 pounds). Size and weight will vary from one design to another.

ANTENNAE FOR INMARSAT C

This system does not support voice. It therefore uses a narrow bandwidth. The transmitter power output is 50 watts, which gives a strong signal with this bandwidth, so a small omnidirectional antenna can be used. The antenna can be approximately 22 centimetres (8.5 inches) in diameter, 32 centimetres (12.5 inches) high and weigh approximately seven kilograms (15.5 pounds). Some makes are as small as 15 x 13 centimetres (6 x 5 inches) and weigh less than one kilogram (2.2 pounds).

MAINTENANCE OF ANTENNAE

All satellite communication antennae are covered and protected by a radome. These need to be kept clean in order to allow radio waves to pass through. Warm soapy water should be used to remove any salt deposits, dirt or soot. It is important not to stand in front of the radome when it is being used, as there is a danger to health. It is therefore imperative to turn off the respective terminal during cleaning to ensure that it is not used. Special paints can now be used on radomes that allow the passage of radio waves.

All terrestrial communication antennae have insulators, which should be kept clean by washing regularly with warm soapy water. They should never be painted. Inspect the insulators for signs of burns or damage, and check all connections, earthing plates and straps.

It is very important that the communications equipment is not used to transmit when maintenance is being carried out, as resulting radiation burns can be horrific. Switch the antenna to ground, if you have this facility, to discharge static.

BATTERIES

Lead acid batteries are the most common source of energy on board. They consist of lead plates surrounded by sulphuric acid mixed with distilled water. On discharge, the chemical reaction between the plates and the electrolyte produces electricity. Great care must always be taken with them, to protect both yourself and your vessel from acid burns and explosion. Hydrogen gas, which is explosive, is produced during charging. If charging continues once the battery is fully charged, the acid will heat up and severe gassing will occur. Many chargers will detect when the battery is fully charged and switch off or reduce to trickle charging, which is often one-tenth of the normal rate. In view of the dangers of hydrogen gas, no machinery in the battery compartment should be capable of producing a spark and the area should be well ventilated at all times.

Marine installations are typically either 12 or 24 volts. The capacity of a battery is usually measured in ampere hours. For example, a one ampere hour battery could produce one amp for one hour, or half an amp for two hours, etc. When batteries are connected in parallel, the total ampere hours is the sum of all the individual batteries' ampere hours.

Rechargeable batteries will always provide better service if they are allowed to fully discharge before fully recharging. Spare batteries are advisable in order to have fully charged batteries available at all times, as required by the radio regulations. Batteries should not be left discharged for long periods of time because there is then a danger that they will fail to recharge.

BATTERY MAINTENANCE

Battery voltage should be tested daily with the battery on load and the charger switched off. First measure the off load voltage. When the battery is put on load, you should not see a drop of more than 10%. Weekly tests should be carried out on reserve sources of energy, for example a motor generator. Monthly tests should involve a thorough inspection of the battery compartment to check the condition of the installation. Always wear goggles and protective clothing when working with batteries. Terminals should be checked for deposits, cleaned and greased. Remove the covers and ensure that the electrolyte is covering the plates. If not, top up with distilled water.

During charging and discharging the specific gravity (relative density) of the electrolyte will change. The density of the electrolyte increases with the charge of the battery, due to lead ions leaving the plates and entering the electrolyte. This is measured in terms of specific gravity and should be checked every month using a hydrometer. The higher the specific gravity, the greater the charge. A reading of approximately 1250 will indicate that the battery is charged, 1150 will indicate that it is discharged. A cell should not be allowed to discharge below 1180. Discharging below a specific gravity reading of 1160 will result in sulphating of the plates.

Maintenance-free batteries have acid within a gel. They cannot be opened but have a small vent on top, which should be kept clear. This type of battery is not suitable for use in areas that are susceptible to frost.

QUESTIONS

1   What type of antenna is required to operate a SAT B terminal?

2   What type of antenna is required to operate a SAT C terminal?

3   You are using your INMARSAT terminal and suddenly lose your communications during an alteration of course. What might have caused this?

4   Why should you keep your whip antenna upright?

5   State the two different ways of installing a wire antenna.

6   What is the purpose of a safety loop?

7   What function does an insulator have?

8   What maintenance should you carry out on your antennae to keep them in peak condition?

9   State the safety precautions that you should observe when maintaining your antennae.

10   What tests should you carry out on your battery installation and when?

11   What are the main dangers associated with a lead acid battery?

12   State the safety precautions that should be observed when dealing with lead acid batteries.

13   Should you test the voltage of a battery when it is on load or off load?

14   What can you deduce from taking a specific gravity reading of the battery's electrolyte?

ANSWERS

1 A large steerable parabolic antenna is required to operate a SAT B terminal.

2 A small omnidirectional antenna is required to operate a SAT C terminal.

3 If you were using your INMARSAT terminal and suddenly lost communications during an alteration of course, it is possible that your antenna has been put into a blind arc.

4 You should keep your whip antenna upright in order to transmit a vertically polarised signal.

5 If the radio installation is amidships, a T installation is used and if the installation is aft, an inverted L installation is used.

6 The weak link is always protected by a safety loop to ensure that the aerial does not fall to the deck and also to maintain its usability.

7 The insulators prevent the wire halyards or deck fittings from forming part of the aerial.

8 Radomes need to be kept clean to allow radio waves to pass through them. Warm soapy water should be used to remove any salt deposits, dirt or soot. All terrestrial communication antennae have insulators, which should be kept clean by washing regularly with warm soapy water. At the time of cleaning, inspect the insulators for signs of burns or damage and check all connections, earthing plates and straps.

9 It is important to ensure that the communications equipment is not capable of being used to transmit when maintenance is being carried out. Switch the antenna to ground if possible.

10 Battery voltage should be tested daily. Weekly tests should be carried out on reserve sources of energy, for example a motor generator. Monthly tests would involve a thorough inspection of the battery compartment to check the condition of the installation. Terminals should be checked for deposits, cleaned and greased. Remove the covers and ensure that the electrolyte is covering the plates. If not, top up with distilled water. Take a specific gravity reading.

11 The main dangers associated with a lead acid battery are explosion of hydrogen gas and acid burns from the electrolyte.

12 Always wear goggles and protective clothing when working with batteries. No machinery in the battery compartment should be capable of producing a spark and the area should be well ventilated at all times.

13 When testing the voltage of a battery it should be on load with the charger switched off.

14 A specific gravity reading of approximately 1250 would indicate that the battery is charged, 1150 would indicate that it is discharged.

Chapter 12

MARITIME SAFETY INFORMATION

NAVTEX

A Navtex co-ordinator collates information from a national warning co-ordinator, a SAR co-ordinator and a meteorological message co-ordinator in order to prepare the Navtex service. Each of these co-ordinators, in turn, is passed information by an array of relevant bodies such as coastguards, buoyage authorities, electronic navaid providers and meteorological offices, making the resulting transmission extremely valuable to mariners. This is a fully automated service that is free of charge to owners of the relevant hardware. A GMDSS Navtex receiver contains duplication of circuitry in order to meet the IMO requirements.

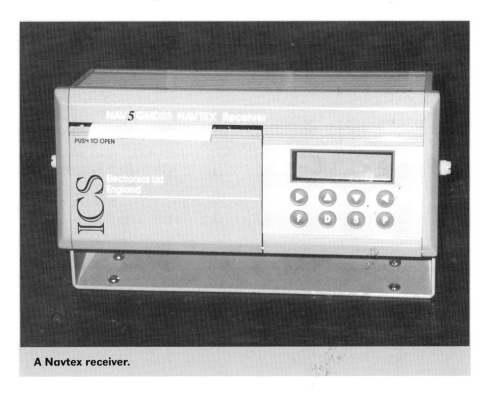

A Navtex receiver.

The range of Navtex is usually within 300 to 400 nautical miles of the transmitting station. Exact details of the range of each individual transmitter may be found in ALRS Volume 5. Greater ranges are possible at night because this is an MF transmission. The English language transmission is received on 518 kHz. Additional local language transmissions may be available on 490 kHz, which is the lowest frequency used in the GMDSS. Because all stations use the same frequency, each one is allocated individual time slots for transmission in order to avoid causing interference to other stations within their range. The exception to this is the issue of gale warnings and SAR information, which may be broadcast at any time. Because of high atmospheric noise levels at 518 kHz, the frequency 4209.5 kHz is used to broadcast MSI in tropical and sub-tropical regions. Once set up, Navtex will work world-wide in any coastal waters offering a Navtex service without modification or additional tuning.

The Navtex unit should be programmed to display or print only messages from stations that are of interest to the user. Providing the Navtex is left switched on, with logging active, repetitions of the same message in the following 72 hours will not be printed. If the roll of thermal paper runs out in the middle of a message, the information will be stored in memory on most units providing the power is not switched off.

A complete list of Navtex stations and their single-letter designators can be found in *ALRS Volume 3* and *5* as well as in other publications.

For the purpose of Navtex, the world is divided into 16 Navareas that are identified by Roman numerals:

I	(1)	United Kingdom	IX	(9)	Pakistan
II	(2)	France	X	(10)	Australia
III	(3)	Spain	XI	(11)	Japan
IV	(4)	USA (east)	XII	(12)	USA (west)
V	(5)	Brazil	XIII	(13)	Russia
VI	(6)	Argentina	XIV	(14)	New Zealand
VII	(7)	South Africa	XV	(15)	Chile
VIII	(8)	India	XVI	(16)	Peru

In addition, each Navarea is divided into A–Z coastal areas (see Figure 27). Within each Navarea there is a selection of transmitting stations that can be chosen. The transmitting stations are used when programming the Navtex receiver. Where there are no Navtex facilities, coastal areas are used when programming for EGC SafetyNET messages. A prime example of this is around Australia.

MESSAGE TYPES

Having programmed the stations, the next task is to decide on the types of messages that are required. Each message type may be either selected or deselected. However, because of their importance, messages A, B and D cannot be deselected and message L should not be deselected.

Opposite: Fig 27 **World-wide Navareas for Navtex.**

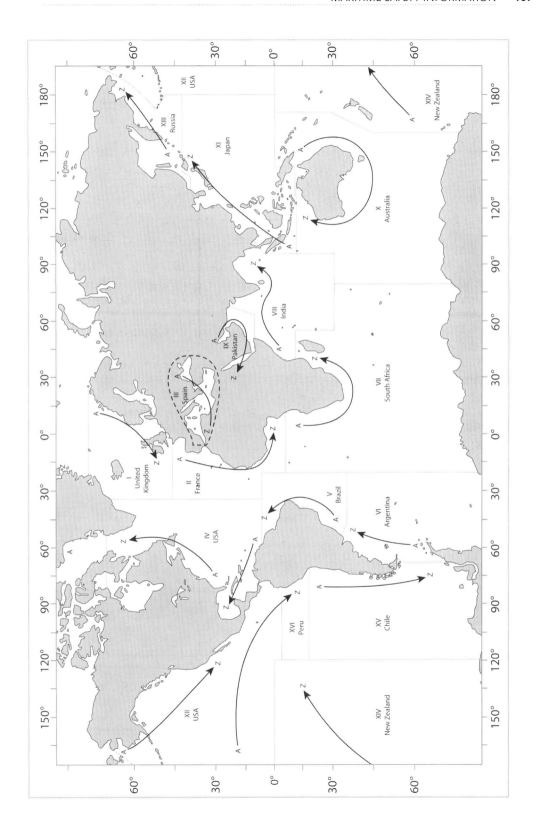

A   Navigational warnings
B   Meteorological warnings
C   Ice reports
D   Search and Rescue information
E   Meteorological forecasts
F   Pilot service messages
G   AIS messages
H   LORAN messages
I   OMEGA messages (now discontinued)
J   SATNAV messages
K   Other electronic navaid messages
L   Navigational warnings in addition to A
V   Special services – trial allocation
W   Special services – trial allocation
X   Special services – trial allocation
Y   Special services – trial allocation
Z   No messages on hand

UK Navtex stations are using V to expand navigational warning information that has been announced under A.

An example of a printout can be seen in Figure 28. The Navtex message has a code, which in this example is EA55. The first letter of the code is the station identification – in this case E is Niton Radio. The second letter is the message type, with A being a navigational warning. The last two digits are the serial number allocated by the station and will always be between 01 and 99. WZ 1061 is a navigational warning code.

NAVTEX MESSAGE   EA55
WZ 1061
ENGLAND SOUTH COAST, ISLE OF WIGHT
ST CATHERINE'S POINT LIGHT 50-35N 001-18W
FIXED RED SECTOR LIGHT UNRELIABLE.

Fig 28 An example of a Navtex navigational warning.

There is a test facility on the unit which candidates should be able to operate. The resultant printout should show that all the characters have been correctly printed and a pass is indicated against each individual test. This does not test the condition of the antenna. If the equipment fails a test, there could be advice in the operator's manual but it is probable that the unit will have to be returned for repair.

An alarm will sound for priority messages. If the Navtex uses paper it will have a visible indication when it is about to run out. To reinsert a new roll, it is advisable to cut the end into a V shape as the task can be awkward. Ensure that the shiny side is uppermost, as this is thermal paper. Once in place, the paper should be advanced by use of the paper feed control. Do not pull the paper through as this can damage the printing head.

FEC

Forward Error Correction is a mode of telex working used by Navtex. This is the broadcast mode, sending a transmission from one station to be received by many. The whole message is sent twice. There are, therefore, only two chances to acquire the correct character. If the character is corrupted the second time, the unit will print a space, question mark or star, depending on the equipment design. The second message is sent slightly behind, but mixed within, the first message. Incoming information will be held in a small memory until it has been received a second time and checked for error.

ENHANCED GROUP CALLING (EGC)

EGC enables information providers that are authorised by IMO to broadcast MSI messages, via LESs and NCSs, to ships fitted with an EGC receiver. SafetyNET is used to distribute meteorological, navigational and search and rescue messages as well as INMARSAT system messages. SafetyNET is the satellite equivalent of the terrestrial Navtex and is also a free service. To receive scheduled navigational warnings for a particular area, the terminal must be logged in to the correct ocean region NCS. When an area is covered by more than one ocean region, only one will be nominated to broadcast the information. Reception is automatic, but the terminal must be pro-grammed with the vessel's current position and the Navarea (not individual stations) and message types that are required. Coastal areas are used around Australia.

The EGC receiver will monitor the NCS common signalling channel that will be used to send EGC messages. Important unscheduled messages are repeated six minutes after the first broadcast to increase the chance of reception. If a station wishes to be able to receive EGC messages at all times, an independent receiver is required.

EGC is most commonly associated with a SAT C terminal. Three types of EGC receiver exist. Class zero is a stand alone receiver. Class two shares a receiver with the communications terminal and will receive EGC messages when communications are not in progress. Class three has two receivers, allowing both of the above operations to take place simultaneously. If the EGC receiver is shared by the SAT C terminal, switching to exclusive EGC mode before a scheduled broadcast will ensure reception of the messages. It is important to switch it back after reception to allow resumption of routine communications.

SAT C terminals will allow the operator to request additional Navareas other than the one that the vessel is in, providing they are covered by the same ocean region. If messages are required for the North Sea, which is Navarea 1, ALRS Volume 5 will advise that this information is available through the Atlantic Ocean Region East satellite at 1730 UTC. For example, if AORW was being used for routine communications, the operator would have to remember to log in to AORE in order to receive the SafetyNET transmission at the appropriate time. Unscheduled broadcasts of SAR information and severe weather warnings will be broadcast on all satellites that serve the area concerned. The advantage of this system over Navtex is that it can be used anywhere within satellite coverage and not just within coastal range of a Navtex transmitter.

The ship's position is usually updated automatically by input from GPS or another position fixing system. Many SAT C terminals are being manufactured with an integral GPS. However, if this is not the case, the position should be updated preferably every four hours, for safety reasons, but at least every 12 hours. After 12 hours, the EGC receiver will assume position information to be lost and print all messages higher than routine for the whole of the ocean region. Operators should print or clear the EGC log regularly to avoid filling the memory.

QUESTIONS

1 On which frequency is the English language Navtex broadcast?

2 What is the approximate range of a Navtex transmission?

3 Why is it important to program the Navtex receiver?

4 Which message types cannot be deselected?

5 What should be checked during your daily tests on the Navtex receiver?

6 What does EGC stand for?

7 What is an EGC SafetyNET message?

8 If your SAT C terminal is not interfaced with a position fixing system, how often should you update the position information?

ANSWERS

1   The English language Navtex messages are broadcast on 518 kHz.

2   The approximate range of a Navtex transmission is 300 to 400 nautical miles, although greater ranges are possible at times.

3   It is important to program the Navtex receiver in order to prevent the printing of messages from stations outside of your area.

4   Message types A, B and D cannot be deselected. L should not be deselected.

    A   Navigational warnings

    B   Meteorological warnings

    D   Search and Rescue information

    L   Navigational warnings in addition to A

5   The Navtex receiver should be checked for an adequate supply of paper during the daily tests.

6   EGC stands for Enhanced Group Calling.

7   An EGC SafetyNET message is the satellite equivalent of a Navtex message.
Messages concerning meteorology, navigation and SAR will be included.

8   If your SAT C terminal is not interfaced with a position fixing system, you should update the position information at least every four hours for safety reasons.

Chapter 13

QUICK REFERENCE GUIDE

Frequencies and their uses

Ch 16	VHF, radiotelephony, distress, urgency, safety and calling.
Ch 06	VHF, radiotelephony, primary intership plus search and rescue.
Ch 08	VHF, radiotelephony, secondary intership.
Ch 13	VHF, radiotelephony, bridge to bridge safety of navigation.
CH 15 and 17	VHF, radiotelephony, on board communications.
Ch 67	VHF, radiotelephony, UK small craft safety.
Ch 70	VHF, DSC, distress, urgency, safety and routine alerting.
490 kHz	MF, Navtex, MSI, second language frequency.
518 kHz	MF, Navtex, MSI in English.
2174.5 kHz	MF, telex, distress, urgency and safety.
2177 kHz	MF, DSC, ship to ship and shore to ship routine alerting.
2182 kHz	MF, radiotelephony, distress, urgency, safety and calling.
2187.5 kHz	MF, DSC, distress, urgency and safety alerting.
2189.5 kHz	MF, DSC, international routine alerting from ship to coast station.
3023 kHz	MF, radiotelephony, aeronautical search and rescue.
8291 kHz	HF, radiotelephony, distress, urgency and safety.
8414.5 kHz	HF, DSC, distress, urgency and safety alerting.
121.5 MHz	Homing signal from some EPIRBs.
406 MHz	COSPAS/SARSAT EPIRB.
1.5/1.6 GHz	INMARSAT
9 GHz	SART.

Signals

The distress signal is a single MAYDAY

The urgency signal is a single PAN PAN

The safety signal is a single SÉCURITÉ

DSC priorities

DISTRESS
DISTRESS RELAY
URGENCY
SAFETY

Example of a distress call

MAYDAY x 3
THIS IS
NAME x 3
CALLSIGN x 1
MMSI x 1

Example of an urgency call

PAN PAN x 3
ALL STATIONS (or an individual station) x 3
THIS IS
NAME x 3
CALLSIGN x 1
MMSI x 1

Example of a safety call

SÉCURITÉ x 3
ALL STATIONS (or an individual station) x 3
THIS IS
NAME x 3
CALLSIGN x 1
MMSI x 1
CHANNEL (or frequency) FOR WORKING
OUT

Example of a distress message

M   MAYDAY
I   IDENTIFICATION - NAME, CALLSIGN AND NUMBER
P   POSITION
N   NATURE OF THE DISTRESS
A   ASSISTANCE REQUIRED
N   NUMBER ON BOARD
O   OTHER INFORMATION
O   OVER

Procedural words used during distress working

By radiotelephony:

SEELONCE MAYDAY used by controlling stations to impose radio silence.

SEELONCE FEENEE used to end radio silence and resume normal working.

The phonetic alphabet

Alpha	**B**ravo	**C**harlie	**D**elta	**E**cho	**F**oxtrot
Golf	**H**otel	**I**ndia	**J**uliet	**K**ilo	**L**ima
Mike	**N**ovember	**O**scar	**P**apa	**Q**uebec	**R**omeo
Sierra	**T**ango	**U**niform	**V**ictor	**W**hiskey	**X**-Ray
Yankee	**Z**ulu				

INMARSAT codes

00 AUTOMATIC DIALLING

32 MEDICAL ADVICE

38 MEDICAL ASSISTANCE OR MEDICAL EVACUATION

39 MARITIME ASSISTANCE

41 METEOROLOGICAL SERVICES

42 NAVIGATIONAL HAZARD REPORTS

43 AMVER SHIP POSITION REPORTS

INDEX